God's Liberating Justice

REVISED EDITION

Grayson Warren Brown

PASTORAL
PRESS
PORTLAND · OREGON

God's Liberating Justice
REVISED EDITION
by Grayson Warren Brown

ISBN 1–56929–070–9

All Scripture quotes are paraphrased.

Pastoral Press
A division of OCP Publications
5536 NE Hassalo Street
Portland, OR 97213–3638

Phone: 1–800–LITURGY (548–8749)
E-mail: *liturgy@ocp.org*
Web: ocp.org

Printed in the United States of America

ABOUT THE AUTHOR

Grayson Warren Brown is a pastoral musician whose music is beloved by many American Catholics. A prolific composer, whose music captures the flavor of traditional Black prayer, Grayson's music has been regarded as a gift to contemporary culture.

He is at once moved with passion about the human condition, yet tempered by experience and a sense of humor. Grayson states that he works out of a general desire to tie together what we do liturgically, as a people gathered to worship, and how we live. He states, "As a liturgist, I feel this book illustrates that the church is not an end in itself—it is rather a means to an end. And the most important concept is that the means is only as good as the end itself. What we do, not who we profess to be, makes us who we are as church."

CONTENTS

Part II

INTRODUCTION & DEDICATION
(to the *First Edition*, 1988)

This may be the first combination introduction/dedication in literary history, but I want to dedicate this book to Bishop Desmond Tutu of South Africa, along with the brave men and women of both Africa and the United States who stand up against apartheid. I also want to use the example of apartheid to introduce this book on Christian justice.

During the time of this writing, the country of South Africa is going through what must be described as a revolution. Her black citizens are beginning to stand up in record numbers, manifesting their unshakable intention to put an end to the racist system of apartheid. Religious leaders, both white and black, in South Africa and around the world are joining together to denounce this racist system. They proclaim it to be a system that stands in contrast to the very laws of God. Bishop Desmond Tutu, a leading civil rights activist and an Episcopal bishop, often cites the Gospels of Jesus as he preaches for a nonviolent end to the unjust laws that are used to keep the black majority oppressed. Pope John Paul II has called for an immediate end to apartheid. Church leaders throughout the United States have marched in protest against the system in South Africa; some have even been arrested for their efforts. And for the first time in years, many of our country's young people have staged demonstrations on college campuses as they called for an end to their universities' investments in South Africa.

And yet, in the face of this, one of the most prominent "religious leaders" of the day recently spoke out in favor of the government of South Africa. Whereas even many conservatives have called for an end to investments in South Africa, this Christian minister has vowed to spend a million dollars to get Americans to buy South African gold and to invest in that country's system. I believe the average Christian has a right to wonder just how there can be such a diversity of opinion on what would seem to be such a clear-cut issue as apartheid, particularly when it comes to Christian consciousness.

1

One might ask, "Does the Bible give us guidelines when it comes to such social issues?" If you look at the vast array of opinions among Christians when it comes to matters of social justice, it might make you wonder if indeed there is any definite view offered in Scripture. It can become rather confusing when so many people believing in one God can act in such opposite extremes.

Another example comes to mind. During the African famine which killed hundreds of thousands of men, women, and children, the Christian organizations banded together to bring food and medicine to the people. When asked why, people often responded that it was indeed the Christian thing to do. It was, as one priest said, "exactly what the Lord commanded his followers to do." At the same time, a television program showed a group of Christians in a church meeting screaming about the blacks and the Jews of America and how they should all be exterminated. They began their meeting with a prayer and closed it with a prayer. They claimed that it was all right to hate Jews because they had discovered that Jesus wasn't actually a Jew, but rather a member of a lost tribe. I'm not sure how they explained Moses, Abraham, Isaiah, Paul, Mary, Martha, James, and others. But the point is that when it comes to social justice issues, there seems to be such a wide variety of thought that it can lead you to wonder if somehow the Scriptures left social thinking up to individual. All this can leave the typical Christian very confused.

But the fact is that the Scriptures are very clear on matters of social justice. What this book is designed to do, therefore, is to offer a historical, biblical perspective regarding such issues as justice, hunger, and racism. I believe the Bible builds a rather convincing argument on the side of people in our society such as Dr. Martin Luther King Jr., Mother Teresa of Calcutta, and Mahatma Gandhi. I also believe it builds a strong case against hatred, racism, and oppression. Consider the story of the Exodus, the works of the prophets, the life and death—and for the Christian, the resurrection—of Jesus. These all build a strong case, historically as well as spiritually, in favor of social justice.

Often, however, much of that view can get lost in this new day of Christian fervor. Words such as "born again" and "evangelize" can begin to take on new and at times distorted meanings if one's faith isn't grounded in Christian ethics. And it would also seem that if love and social justice are not deeply a part of that ethic, then we have indeed lost something in the translation between the Word and our faith.

This book is meant to offer a biblical viewpoint on the topic of love and justice. It is not meant to be the last word, but I hope it will encourage those who read it to want to know more. I hope it leaves no doubt whatsoever that matters of hunger, oppression, and love are all part of the very nature of this God that Jesus called Father.

Last, I chose to end this book with some personal thoughts on the Scriptures. I do so because I would hope that those reading this work would be encouraged to do some independent study. However, I know that for many, just picking up a Bible and reading it can sometimes create more questions than answers.

INTRODUCTION
(to the *Revised Edition*, 2005)

What is Justice?

Several years ago when I wrote the first edition of this book, a wondrous and glorious event was happening in the world. Under the leadership of such people as African Episcopal Bishop Desmond Tutu and civil rights leader Nelson Mandela, apartheid was coming to an end and the people of South Africa were finally breaking free from years of torturous oppression. I find it most interesting that the majority of those who led the movement were Christian, bringing to this struggle a biblical view of justice that was totally void of violence. There were no cries from these leaders—once freedom was won—for vengeance upon those who had kept so many people locked in a cruel and murderous system. There was extraordinary talk of mercy and forgiveness on the lips of the victims of this systematic oppression and persecution which sometimes led to death.

Several years later, an act of domestic terrorism rocked this nation. On April 19, 1995, the Alfred P. Murrah federal building in Oklahoma City was blown up, killing 168 men, women, and children and injuring 850 people. A young man, Timothy McVeigh was apprehended, tried, and convicted for this brutal act. He was ultimately sentenced to death and was executed by lethal injection on June 11, 2001.

A reporter began asking people what they thought should happen to the man convicted of this murderous act. One by one, the people interviewed said they thought he should be put to death, but one man said no. He said that even though he had lost a granddaughter in the blast, and she had meant more to him than anyone could ever imagine, he still did not want to see the man responsible put to death. The reporter looked at him in disbelief and asked the man if he wanted to see justice done. The man, in return, asked what justice would be served by adding yet another death to this already tragic situation. He said killing the man responsible would not bring back his granddaughter, but would simply leave yet another set of parents mourning the death of a child. When asked how he could respond like this, the man replied, "I am a Christian."

A man is being stoned to death, rocks pelting him from every side. He is an innocent man, at least innocent of any serious crime. (He was guilty of pointing out the hypocrisy of those who believed they were too blessed to have to change their hearts.) Battered and bruised and near death, Stephen raises his eyes toward the heavens, and instead of asking that this brutal act be avenged, he cries out to Jesus in words echoing Christ's own words to his Father when he was about to die. He says,

> "Lord, don't hold this against them." (Acts of the Apostles 7:60)

A young Episcopal priest pastors a church three blocks from the World Trade Center on September 11, 2001. Upon meeting him at his church just three days after the attack, I am struck by the sense of peace and joy on his face and in his heart. He tells me that the windows of nearly every building in the area were blown out when the twin towers fell, yet not single pane of glass was broken at two hundred-year-old Church of St. Paul. His church becomes a command center for volunteers working long hours to help bring some healing to those whose lives were so traumatically disrupted. All over the church banners are displayed from people around the world, pledging their support and solidarity with the citizens of New York and the United States. What is missing is the very understandable sense of anger and outrage felt by so many people. Instead, the pastor's words are all about the amazing stories of individuals who are doing the healing work of God—and how we should pray for those who did this terrible act.

> In the face of such evil, he dares to take seriously the words, "Forgive us our debts, as we also forgive our debtors." (Matthew 6:12)

These views and actions seem to stand in stark contrast to the way so much of our contemporary world runs. Today when people speak of justice, they often mean vengeance. And far too often, people equate forgiveness with weakness. The problem with strength through vengeance is that one can become locked into a never-ending cycle of retaliation—producing more and more violence, hatred, and even death—not only the death of individuals, but the death of reason as well. All who believe that entering into a constant cycle of bombings and killings will eventually bring about lasting peace have not only lost their hearts, they've also lost their minds.

What does Scripture tell us about love and justice? One thing it tells us that we can never have real peace unless there is justice in society. The next thing it tells us is that justice in biblical terms is not vengeance, but the word justice is more closely associated with acts of charity, like taking care of the poor, the hungry, the homeless, the widows, and the orphans. Scripture makes very clear that as long as we neglect the needs of the poorest of the poor in our world, true and lasting peace can never be really achieved.

The other message Scripture tells us is that contrary to all one might believe, mercy and forgiveness are not tools of the weak, but weapons of the strong. It would take little for the black South Africans to want to kill their white oppressors after years of apartheid. Nor would it take much for the Oklahoma grandfather to want to avenge the death of his granddaughter. Likewise Stephen would have had true earthly justification for wanting God to punish those who were taking his life.

Believing in the power of forgiveness and mercy when one has been wronged takes something beyond mere human ability. It means recognizing the limitations of human nature, and tapping into the awesome and unlimited power of God.

This book is divided into two parts. The first part looks at the Old Testament and examines examples of justice as the ancient Hebrews understood it. It looks into the covenant agreement between God and Hebrews during the Exodus experience, showing how it shaped the view of the Jewish people toward the poor, the hungry, and those who were oppressed. It then moves through the Prophets, into the New Testament, and Jesus' continuation of the justice motif, adding elements of love and mercy.

The second part of the book looks into the Bible itself and examines the different personalities of God as seen in the Old Testament and the New Testament, offering some possible reasons for the apparent changes. It also seeks to explore the dangers in not recognizing the times and customs of the earlier scripture writers.

> "But judgment shall be revealed as water, and justice as a mighty torrent." (Amos 5:23)

> "I will show you what is good, and what the LORD requires of you: only to do justice, to love mercy, and to walk humbly with your God." (Micah 6:8)

Part I

From Freedom to Oppression

In order to best understand the biblical writings dealing with justice and oppression, it is necessary to begin with a short history of the Israelites and how they became an oppressed people in the land of Egypt. The accounts in Genesis and Exodus are filled with historical facts, political insight, and a keen view of human and political nature. How much of this story is also filled with tribal legends and professions of faith is not important at this point, it is something to be addressed later in this work. What is important is that these early scripture writers wanted to paint a very clear picture of the relationship between God, oppression, justice, and society. The story of Joseph in Egypt (Genesis 37–50) sets the stage for the eventual bondage of the Israelites by the Egyptians, their release by God, and the subsequent writings on justice in the law by the Prophets.

Joseph in Egypt

According to Scripture, there lived a man named Jacob who had many sons, but favored one named Joseph. Out of jealousy, the other sons conspired to kill their favored brother. However, one son intervened and they decided to sell Joseph into slavery to a group of Midianites. The Midianites in turn sold Joseph to a captain of the guard in Pharaoh's army, and the captain took Joseph to Egypt. Like many of the early Old Testament writings, the Scriptures tell a rather earthy story that has all the elements of a modern-day soap opera.

It seems as though the Egyptian captain came to take quite a liking to the young man he had bought to be his slave, and began to turn more and more of the household responsibilities over to Joseph. In fact, things were going so well that Potiphar (the Egyptian captain) eventually put him in charge of his entire estate.

> " . . . Joseph found favor in the sight of Potiphar, and ministered to him: being set over all by him, he governed the house committed to him, and all things that were delivered to him."
> (Genesis 39:4)

However, there was one slight problem. It seems as though "Mrs. Potiphar" also began to take a special liking to the young man, but for different reasons. Joseph apparently was a rather good-looking, strapping young man, and the captain's wife took quite a fancy to him, so much so that she tried to seduce him. And the Scriptures leave nothing to the imagination when it comes to revealing her intentions.

> "And after many days his mistress cast her eyes on Joseph, and said: 'Lie with me.'" (Genesis 39:6)

Joseph, in a non-too-tactful manner rebuffs her advances, stating that her husband trusted him, and he would never betray that trust. But the wife was not about to be put off so easily. One day while the servants were out of the house, Joseph went inside to attend to his duties. Once inside, the captain's wife grabbed him and tried to have her way with him. He again rebuffed her and ran out of the house, leaving his cloak in her grasp.

> "Now it happened on a certain day, that Joseph went into the house, and was doing some business without any man with him. And catching his garment, she said, 'Lie with me.' But he, leaving the garment in her hand, fled, and went out."
> (Genesis 39:11–12)

This infuriated the captain's wife. She decided that if she could not have him, she would tell her husband and the servants that Joseph had tried to force himself on her.

> "And when the woman saw the garment in her hands, and herself disregarded, she called to her the men of her house, and said to them, 'See, he has brought in a Hebrew to abuse us; he came in to me, to lie with me, and when I cried out, he heard my voice and left the garment that I held, and got him out.'
>
> For a proof therefore of her fidelity, she kept the garment and showed it to her husband when he returned home. She said, 'The Hebrew servant whom you brought, came to me to abuse me. And when he heard me cry, he left the garment which I held and fled out.' His master hearing these things and giving too much credit to his wife's words was very angry. He cast Joseph into the prison where the king's prisoners were kept, and he was imprisoned there." (Genesis 39:13–20)

I think it is most interesting that from the very beginning of Scripture, we see a relationship develop between God and real-life people, in real-life human situations. This is a book about God and real life.

We pick up the story again in Pharaoh's prison, where Joseph was imprisoned. The Egyptian Pharaoh had a very disturbing dream that even his wise men were unable to interpret satisfactorily. Pharaoh's butler, who had spent some time with Joseph in prison (for what we don't quite know), told the Pharaoh of an extraordinary young man with a talent for reading dreams who (at that very time) was a prisoner in Pharaoh's jail. The Pharaoh sent for Joseph, who immediately deciphered the dream, thus saving Egypt from imminent famine and thereby winning the Pharaoh's favor. The Pharaoh was so grateful for Joseph's service to the country that he freed him and made him viceroy over all of Egypt. This made Joseph the second most-powerful man in the land. Here again, Scripture takes us through another series of plot twists that eventually lead to the reconciliation of Joseph with his brothers and family.

Under Joseph and this particular Pharaoh, Jews were allowed to immi-grate to Egypt, buy land and cattle, and settle peacefully. The end of the book of Genesis and the opening of the book of Exodus tells of the permanent settlements by Joseph's family, the different households of Jacob, and of the prosperity they enjoyed in Egypt. It also becomes obvious that times in Egypt were changing drastically. As the book of Exodus opens, we learn that Joseph is now dead, as is his kindly patron, the Pharaoh. The Israelites were now firmly entrenched in Egypt and many of them were doing quite well. However, not all is well in the land of Egypt.

> "The children of Israel increased and were fruitful, they grew strong they filled the land." (Exodus 1:7)

We learn next in Exodus that a new dynasty has come to power (more than likely by force). Here it is necessary to understand how various dynasties came to power in ancient Egypt.

Unlike the popular Hollywood versions of Egyptian history, power was not always handed down from father to son in a neat family ritual. Power was often taken either by different factions within Egypt itself, or by outside forces that would invade and rule. Egyptian history suggests that, at times, there were several kings simultaneously ruling different parts of Egypt, often prompting wars within its borders. Several historians hold the same theory: Most likely, the Pharaoh of Joseph's time was a member of a foreign occupying power from Asia, known as the Hyksos. It seems as though when they conquered Egypt, the country (because of infighting) was too divided to defend itself. When this powerful Asian army attacked, they were able to conquer Egypt and then place one of their own leaders on the throne, giving Egypt a foreign-born Pharaoh. The theory is further borne out by the idea of Joseph, a foreigner, being appointed to such a powerful position as viceroy. It is generally believed that no Egyptian would ever appoint a foreigner to such an important position, no matter how great they were—unless of course, the Pharaoh himself was from another land.

It is believed that after years of occupation, Egyptian forces banded together and overthrew the Hyksos' rule, bringing a new dynasty to power. The leader of this insurrection would then set himself as the new Pharaoh. This new regime probably needed to win the confidence of the Egyptian people. They also might have feared that the old dynasty would call upon the Israelites, whom they had always treated fairly, to help them regain power in Egypt. Therefore, the new Pharaoh decided to rally the people around a "common enemy," the Israelites. It is important, however, to see that the oppression that followed was the result of both political and economic expediency as well as hatred and bigotry.

"In the meantime there arose a new king over Egypt that didn't know Joseph. And he said to his people, 'These people of the children of Israel are numerous and stronger than we are. We need to wisely oppress them so that they don't increase too much. If they do and a war shall rise against us, they will join with our enemies and defeat us, taking control of our land.'" (Exodus 1:8–10)

Once again contained in this passage is the strong suggestion that this Pharaoh was not from the same household as the old Pharaoh. The idea that the new Pharaoh was one who "didn't know Joseph" would suggest that the Pharaoh was either in exile or at least not near the seat of power in Egypt. The idea that he speaks to his people in such a manner clearly implies, considering how the story unfolds, that he is an Egyptian speaking to Egyptians about the legacy of a foreign dynasty imposing its will upon a sovereign people.

Much like Hitler did in the late 1930's in Germany, the new Pharaoh probably consolidated his power using some basic tactics for oppression—fierce nationalism, along with the basic mistrust of things done by the occupying administration, and suspicion of "outsiders" taking over the country, stealing goods and power away from the indigenous "rightful" owners of the land's resources. History goes on to show that the Israelites' status in society became more and more threatened. Suspicion turned into fear, violence, and finally oppression. Isaac Asimov writes:

"This sort of thing feeds on itself. The Israelites, treated like second-class citizens and as objects of suspicion, become disaffected and this disaffection is itself the excuse for intensified oppression. The oppressor, rightly fearing the resentment of the oppressed, finds discrimination escalating into slavery almost automatically." (*Asimov's Guide to the Bible—Two Volumes in One—The Old and New Testaments,* [NY: Random House, 1981], p. 121)

By the time we get to the account of the actual exodus, the status of the Israelites has deteriorated into slavery. The Jews are now an oppressed people in Egyptian society, totally without rights or protection. It is to these people that God will reveal his feelings on justice and oppression.

The Covenant Agreement

It is in the book of Exodus that we begin to see a pattern develop and God's view on matters of injustice and oppression starts to unfold. We see God make a covenant agreement with an enslaved people. He recognizes their plight and sees that they are living under a system that is cruel and oppressive. Furthermore, he sees that they are without any of the basic human rights that are meant to be given to all of his children, seeing that they are slaves, considered second class, and are forced to serve others without compensation or dignity. Because it appears God cannot tolerate such injustice, he calls one from among them, Moses, and through Moses, God delivers a powerful message.

> "Say to the children of Israel, I am the LORD who will bring you out from the work prison of the Egyptians, and will deliver you from slavery, and redeem you with arm lifted high and great acts of judgment. And I will take and adopt you to be my people and I will be your God. You shall know that I am the LORD your God, who freed you from slavery under the Egyptians." (Exodus 6:6–7)

As the story of the exodus unfolds, it becomes clear that in God's action is the requirement that the Israelites as a society, once free, must live in such a way that would reveal to all the principles and nature of this liberation by God. Although the Bible narrative does not make crystal clear when or how this understanding fully develops between God and the chosen, it does make clear the point that the Jewish people saw this concept as being integral to the covenant agreement. Let's examine the terms of this covenant as understood by the chosen.

God chooses to adopt an oppressed people, and he says to them that he, the LORD, will personally enter into their struggle to be free. He says that once they are free from their bondage they must write laws and codes that will promote justice and freedom, both for themselves and for those not of their own race.

He makes it clear to them that they must treat everyone fairly because they know what it means to be treated unjustly. God states that once they were free and in their own land:

> "You shall not oppress the stranger, for you know what it feels like to be a stranger, as you were strangers in Egypt." (Exodus 23:9)

The Israelites believed that they were being given a mandate by God— that in effect said, 'Together, you and I will show all future generations that oppression, injustice, hatred, and bigotry are all things disgusting in my sight. You and I will make it clear to all coming generations that justice and righteousness are more important to me than ten thousand acts of worship and that I will never abide oppression and callousness.'

And so we see in Exodus that God and his chosen people took on all the powers of a mighty empire and emerged victorious. The Israelites escaped Pharaoh's tyranny and set out for the Promised Land. Once they had escaped their oppression, God reminded them that they and their LORD were in a partnership. He continued to remind them of what he had done for them and what he expected from them in return.

> "You have seen what I have done to the Egyptians, how I have carried you upon eagle's wings, and have brought you to myself. If you will only hear my voice and keep my covenant, you shall be mine above all people . . ." (Exodus 19:4–5)

God kept his side of the bargain. Now it was up to the Israelites, and at first the people tried to live up to their part of the agreement. While they traveled together in the desert, they began to formulate laws that would ensure that they would live free from injustice and oppression. Even poverty, which is often a sign of a society's indifference for one another, was dealt with in the laws. Specifications were made in the law and Holiness Codes to provide for the poor, so that their rights would be guaranteed. The books of

Exodus, Leviticus, and Deuteronomy all contain excellent attempts, by law, to ensure that the bargain would be kept. Even though much of the law dealt with such issues as cleanliness and religious ritual, it also dealt strongly with the rights of the poor, the oppressed, and the alien.

> "If you lend money to any of my people that are poor, you shall not be hard upon them as an extortioner, nor oppress them with interest charges." (Exodus 22:25)

> "If you take your neighbor's garment in pawn, you shall give it back to him before sunset, because that garment is his only covering. It is the garment in which he covers himself, and he has nothing else to sleep in." (Exodus 22:26–27a)

> "You shall not deprive a poor man of justice." (Exodus 23:6)

> "You shall not oppress your neighbor, nor oppress him by violence. The wages of those you've hired should not be kept from them until the next morning. You shall not speak bad of the deaf, nor put a stumbling block before the blind." (Leviticus 19:13–14a)

> "If a stranger dwells in your land, and abides among you, do not oppress him. But let him be among you as a native of your country, and you shall love him as yourselves, for you were strangers in the land of Egypt. I am the LORD your God. Do not do any unjust thing in judgment, in rule, in weight, or in measure." (Leviticus 19:33–35)

> "And when you reap your land's harvest, you shall not cut it to the very ground; neither shall you gather the fallen ears of corn that remain; but you shall leave them for the poor and for the strangers." (Leviticus 23:22)

> "Cursed be the one that withholds justice from the stranger, of the orphan and the widow." (Deuteronomy 27:19)

"Do fair judgment to the fatherless and the widow, love the stranger, and give him food and clothing. Therefore love strangers, because you also were strangers in the land of Egypt." (Deuteronomy 10:18–19)

"Do not withhold justice from the stranger or the fatherless; neither shall you take away the widow's cloak as a pledge. Remember that you were slaves in Egypt, and the LORD your God delivered you from there. I command you to do this thing." (Deuteronomy 24:17–18)

From these passages it is clear that the Jewish people who were once captive are now free from oppression (with God's help), and are to treat other people with charity, as they, themselves were victims of poverty and oppression in the same manner. It was clear that no matter how wealthy members of the community became, they still had an obligation to the poor and the alien. All of these commands came with the constant reminder that they (themselves) had been recipients of God's mercy, and were therefore expected to show the same kind of generosity to the less fortunate members of their communities. The poor were not to be treated with hostility or contempt, but were to be treated in the same way God had treated them—with love, mercy, and charity. This theme would repeat itself (in various forms) throughout the whole Bible narrative.

It is interesting to note that while the Jewish people were in a semi-nomadic state, their concern for one another and with the laws regarding the poor seemed to be of the highest concern. However, once the chosen settled into the new land, started acquiring property and power, and began to rule, something else began to happen. Many of these people, who, only a few generations before, had been the victims of oppression, began to oppress their fellow citizens. The covenant agreement was broken not by God but by his chosen people.

The Prophets

For those who remembered the covenant, seeing the people with whom God had made this agreement acting like the oppressive people from whom he had liberated them, was more than they could bear. Men such as Jeremiah, Amos, and Isaiah burst onto the scene and their message was often the same. They cried out that the chosen, the Israelites, had entered into an agreement with God, and that living justly was essential to that agreement.

The prophets believed that, after the exodus experience, there should never again have been any doubt about God's view relative to what was just and what was unjust. When God spoke about justice, the definition was clear; when God spoke about the oppressed, the definition again was clear. Oppression of the poor, the weak, the hungry, and society's powerless were the very things that God had fought against along with the Israelites' fathers and mothers. All the chosen had to do was to remember their position in Egyptian society when God entered into the covenant with them. The prophets warned that no amount of prayer or sacrifice could act as a substitute for the just society that had been promised to God. Without that justice, the Israelites were living in a manner contrary to the will of the Almighty.

From the earliest works of Scripture we find that God is not only concerned with personal (one-on-one) justice, but with societal justice as well. Perhaps that is why it was so important that the Jews enter into an agreement that included a code of behavior by which the whole community would live. We learn from the prophets that it was not only individuals who turned away from God by refusing to do justice, but it was a people—an "Israel"—who did "bruise the heads of the poor upon the earth."

> "For three crimes of Israel, and for four I will not convert them, because they sold the just one for silver, and the poor man for a pair of shoes. They bruise the heads of the poor upon the dust of the earth, and turn aside the humble..."
> (Amos 2:6–7)

The prophets cried out against all the corruption and exploitation of the poor by the (now rich and powerful) Israelites. Indeed, justice was the central theme of most of their work. They kept warning the Israelites that being chosen carried with it not just honor, but responsibility as well. Part of that responsibility was to adopt God's code of love and justice as their code of behavior toward one another (indeed, toward all people), just as wholeheartedly as God had adopted them to be his chosen.

Should any have wanted to know "Who is this God of Israel?"—according to the agreement, they should have been able to look at the chosen and their society and know. The Israelites should have reflected that he was a kind, understanding God who loved everyone the same, cared equally for all people, and had special concern about the needs of the poor. Above all, they should have been able to discern that God was loving, just, and hated oppression and poverty. However, when they looked at those that had been freed by God, they did not see this representation of God's presence. Instead, as time passed, they began to see a people who had forgotten their heritage. Some had become very rich and powerful, and began to exploit those who were less fortunate. For example, the Northern Kingdom, under the reign of King Jeroboam II, attained tremendous prosperity, although few were able to share in this wealth. A handful lived in luxury, while at the same time, the poor were treated terribly, and some were even sold into slavery.

The prophets protested vehemently. They saw a society proclaiming supreme allegiance to this God of justice, and yet running contrary to his precepts. They saw a court system where justice for the rich and justice for the poor were no longer equal. They saw corruption in business. They saw the poor and the powerless (particularly widows and orphans, the least powerful) ignored by society. They saw oppression of the poor by practically everyone who had power. As stated before, with God, societal justice is as important as individual justice, particularly in the case of any society or people who claim to be close to him.

The grievance that the prophets had with the chosen centered around the fact that the Israelites no longer seemed to care that oppression and poverty flourished in their midst, contrary to the agreement their ancestors had struck with God who set them free. Again and again, the prophets cried out: How could a people so close to God and who, themselves, had suffered tremendous injustice, in turn oppress others? The prophets kept calling the Israelites' attention back to the covenant agreement, often ending their discourses with the reminder:

"It is I that brought you out of Egypt…" (cf. Jeremiah 2:6–7; Amos 2:10; Micah 6:4)

The prophets kept saying—God kept saying, "You, as a people, know what it's like to be a minority—poor, oppressed, derided, ridiculed, and forced to always serve—you were there. I heard your cry and delivered you." Because this God was perceived as a God who stood against oppression, he had to respond to the Israelites' injustice as he had responded to the Egyptians' injustice. As the psalmist would later proclaim:

"The LORD hath made known his salvation; he has revealed his justice . . ." (Psalm 98:2)

As we examine how the writings and preaching of the prophets specifically pertain to justice, it is important to note how they equate the turning away from social justice with turning away from God. In fact, they felt that the great destruction of the kingdom would result, in part, because of the inequality and injustice that existed. This is how the prophets saw the society composed of the people freed from oppression by God:

"Assemble yourselves upon the mountains of Samaria, and behold the many follies in your midst and those that suffer oppression . . . and they have not known to do the right thing, says the LORD, storing in their houses what they have gained through iniquity and robbery." (Amos 3:9–10)

The prophets spoke directly to different elements of society and tried to warn them of the dangers of building a society based on injustice. They spoke (rather unflatteringly) to the rich women of the city:

"Hear this word, you women in the mountains of Samaria, you that oppress the needy and crush the poor, that say to your masters, 'Bring us drink!' The Lord GOD has sworn by his holiness that your time is coming when they shall lift you up on their shields." (Amos 4:1–2)

They spoke to the rulers of the city about the injustice of their leadership:

"Hear this, you princes of the house of Jacob, and you judges of the house of Israel: you that abhor judgment and corrupt all that is right; you that build up Zion with blood and Jerusalem with iniquity. Her rulers have judged for bribes and her priests have taken bribes for their spiritual direction, and her prophets divined for money, yet they rely on the LORD, saying, 'Is not the LORD in the midst of us?' then they say, 'no evil shall come upon us.'" (Micah 3:9–11)

They spoke of all those who made their fortunes while at the same time either oppressing the poor or simply doing nothing to stop the injustice:

". . . they become great and grand, and grow gross and fat, and have evil thoughts. They refuse to do justice, and have ignored the cause of widows and orphans, and don't treat the poor with justice. 'Should I punish them for this?' says the LORD." (Jeremiah 5:27b–29a)

They spoke out against the elders and their officers for their treatment of the poor:

"The Lord will enter into judgment with the elders of his people, and their princes; you have devoured the vineyard, and the spoils of the poor are in your house. Why do you consume my people, and grind the faces of the poor?" (Isaiah 3:14–15a)

They spoke out against a court system that favored the rich and powerful over the poor and powerless:

"You that upend judgment and forsake justice in the land, you hate him that brings a wrongdoer to court and abhor him that speaks the truth. This is because you robbed the poor, and took the choice grain from them." (Amos 5:7, 10, 11ab)

The prophets spoke so strongly because they believed that a God of justice would be quite simply dismayed at the lack of justice among his chosen.

"The vineyard of the LORD of hosts is Israel and the men of Judah are the plant he cherished. He looked for justice in judgment but found bloodshed outcries of distress." (Isaiah 5:7)

Let Justice Roll down Like a Mighty River

To the prophets, justice is not only a concern of God; it is part of the very essence of God. The author Abraham Heschel observes:

> "There are few thoughts as deeply ingrained in the mind of biblical man as the thought of God's justice and righteousness. It is not an inference, but an *a priori* of biblical faith, self-evident; not an added attribute to his essence, but given with the very thought of God. It is inherent in his essence and identified with his ways." (*The Prophets* [New York: Colophon Books, 1962], p. 199–200)

So, to the prophets and the early scripture writers, injustice and oppression were considered to be against the very nature and makeup of God. This is an extremely important point when examining a relationship between a God whose very essence is justice and a people who are only marginally interested in that justice. Matters of hunger, poverty, racism, and oppression are not issues that should merely *concern* the believer; they are matters that should be ever-present in the heart and mind of the believer.

The prophets believed that merely giving to a charity or refraining from overt oppression of the poor was not enough. You are called to actively defend the poor, the oppressed, and the helpless. You are called to:

> ". . . seek justice and take the cause of the oppressed, judge for the orphans and defend the widow's cause." (Isaiah 1:17bc)

Knowing God

Perhaps one of the most powerful thoughts the prophets instilled in the minds of those around them was the concept of "knowing God." The prophets felt that for one to believe in God and not acknowledge the importance of justice was really not to know God at all. They would constantly ask how anyone could know the God of justice and still hate people who were poor, alien, or different. They would ask how anyone could know God and yet do nothing to help those who were less fortunate. To live a life unaffected by the oppression and suffering of others left you, in the eyes of the prophets, filled with ignorance (if not downright contempt for God), and thus deserving of whatever calamity he might choose to befall you or your whole town. Social justice was simply that important in the Old Testament.

To the prophets it didn't matter how much power, wealth, or status someone had in society; in matters concerning love, justice, and the Lord, the message was that God was a God of justice and love. He was a God who stood for freedom over oppression and who would always hear the cries of those who were oppressed. If people wanted to be on the right side of God, they would have to know God; part of knowing God was to put his precepts above everything else. Perhaps one of the most beautiful verses in all the prophetic writing comes from Jeremiah when he speaks on this very issue:

> "The LORD says, Let not the wise man boast of his wisdom, and let not the strong man glory in his strength; let not the rich man glory in his riches; but if he boasts, let him boast of this, that he understands and knows me. I am the LORD that exercises mercy, judgment, and justice on the earth; for these things please me, says the LORD." (Jeremiah 9:22–24)

A Working Definition

I emphasize all this so early in this work because we need a good working knowledge of justice in scriptural terms. After this I will simply use the words "justice" and "righteousness" to explore issues. For now it is only important that we understand how justice in Scripture is at the very core of the things that afflict people unfairly. The justice of God is intricately tied to the poor, the hungry, the oppressed, and the powerless. The same God, who chose to free a people from the oppression of the Egyptians, challenged them to free others whom they in turn had oppressed. This God who chose to be known for this love and justice asks (or, as the prophets would say, demands) that all those who choose freely to follow him be fully involved in bringing justice into an often unjust world. The prophets of the Old Testament spoke in threats, in pleas, in anger, and in sorrow, but their theme was often the same: seek justice; do justice; live justice; and stand for justice. When it comes to the God of Israel, justice is literally more important than anything.

How Important is Justice?
If You Obey, and Only If You Obey . . .

Through Jeremiah, the LORD speaks to the king of Judah and warns him and his people about impending destruction. But God also explains the condition under which the city can yet be saved; the LORD is talking about the bottom line, so to speak. As we move further along through Scripture, it is interesting to note how often in both the New and Old Testaments this issue becomes the "bottom line." When scripture writers reach this point, love and justice are most often the central theme:

> "Go down to the house of the King of Judah, and say this, 'Hear the word of the LORD, O King of Judah, that sits on the throne of David, you and your servants, and your people, who enter through these gates.' These are the LORD'S words, 'Exercise judgment and justice, and rescue the oppressed from the oppressor, and don't mistreat strangers, orphans, and widows; don't shed innocent blood in this place. If you will do this thing, then shall there enter in by the gates of this house, kings of the lineage of David sitting upon his throne, and riding in chariots and on horses, they and their servants, and their people. But if you will not listen to my words, I swear by myself, says the LORD, that this house shall become desolate." (Jeremiah 22:1–5)

What you have here is the LORD speaking to the very people he has loved, nurtured, and freed from their own oppression. He reminds them that injustice strikes at the very root of God. In the very next passage you hear a God speak with an almost remorseful heart, warning his people about what he would be either forced to do, as the prophet understood it, or perhaps powerless to prevent because of the injustice of these, his covenant people.

> "Though you are as dear to me as Gilead or as the heights of Lebanon, yet surely I will make you a wilderness, and cities not habitable." (Jeremiah 22:6bc)

The prophets believed that when justice was denied and injustice was allowed to run rampant, then the covenant agreement was broken and God was under attack (cf. Matthew 25:45). Since all that is in God's nature is under attack, the prophets felt that God could simply no longer protect his people from the violence and injustice of the world, or worse yet, that he would become angry and fight back.

Nevertheless, history repeated itself; just as the hearts of the Pharaoh and the Egyptians were hardened against justice, so the hearts of the chosen were hardened. In 587 B.C., the Babylonians destroyed the great kingdom of Judah. What that meant to the people of Israel was the destruction of the heart and soul of their very being. Unlike a democracy or republic, these people lived under a theocracy (the belief that God was the center of their civic as well as their religious life). The symbol of that theocracy was the temple. What signaled the awful destruction of Judah was the destruction of the holy temple, thus signaling, in a very real sense, the removal of God from their midst.

Worship, Liturgy, and Justice

Once you begin to see how important a loving and just society is to the God of Israel, you can better understand the absolute fury the prophets showed when it came to matters of worship by a people who denied justice. Here the prophets took dead aim; their position was clear. They said that without social justice, worship was a farce. Praying, singing, sacrificing, and uttering "holy words" all meant very little when those involved treated their brothers and sisters poorly. In fact, these actions were actually offensive to God. You get the sense that the prophets were taking on an age-old problem, one that would exist for centuries.

They questioned how anyone could refuse to do the will of God by living with the prejudice and oppression that existed, yet still maintain the trappings of a true believer. The prophets believed that simply going through the rituals of worship did not mean that you were honest or sincere in your belief. They realized that the best way to praise God was to do his will. But if one were either actually involved somehow in the oppression of one's neighbors or simply allowed it to happen without stopping it, then that person's sacrificing and fasting were not acceptable to the God of Israel.

What we learn from the prophets about justice and worship is that worship is never accepted as a substitute for justice. If, therefore, people entered the house of the Lord with prayer and sacrifices, but continued to leave the temple only to treat others with contempt or to use them in greed, then the prophets considered their worship hypocritical and empty. Again, this thought bears repeating. In order to worship God you were called to know God; and to know God was to do justice, particularly toward the poor and needy. Jesuit Father John R. Donahue, in his essay "Biblical Perspectives on Justice" speaks about Jeremiah's praise for King Josiah (one of the few kings Jeremiah was ever known to praise):

"He is the one who 'knew' Yahweh, and the knowing of Yahweh is taking the cause of the poor and needy. Here there is no division between *theroia* and *praxis*, between faith and doing justice. Justice is concrete. It combines non-exploitation of the poor with taking their cause. The doing of justice is not the application of religious faith, but its substance, without knowing it, God remains unknown." (*The Faith that Does Justice*, John C. Haughey, ed. [New York: Paulist Press, 1977], p. 76)

Prayer is important and sacrifice is important; but without justice they are simply empty words and empty symbols. The prophets make this crystal clear again and again. All the prayers and sacrifices in the world won't make up for a lack of social concern and justice. Some of the strongest words spoken by the Old Testament prophets are said in relation to the notion of liturgy, worship, and the lack of social justice.

"I hate. I have rejected your festivities; and I will not receive your sacred ceremonies. And if you offer me sacrifices and gifts, I will not receive them; neither will I regard the shared offerings of your beasts. Take away from me the sound of your songs; I will not hear the canticles of your harp. But judgment shall be revealed as a rolling river, and justice as a mighty torrent." (Amos 5:21–24)

Ceremony, ritual sacrifice, and fasting—all become abominations in God's sight when justice is missing. It is hard to misunderstand the intensity of God's purpose and resolve when it comes to ritual and worship without the presence of justice.

"Offer sacrifices no more in vain, incense is an abomination to me . . . And when you stretch forth your hands, I will turn away my eyes from you; and when you offer countless prayers, I will not listen, for your hands have blood on them. Wash yourselves and be clean, put the evil of your deeds away from my eyes. Cease to do evil and learn to do good. Seek judgment, relieve the oppressed, and plead for the orphan and the widow." (Isaiah 1:13, 15–17)

Interestingly, in the footnotes of *The New English Bible, Oxford Study Edition*, this passage is labeled simply "Instruction on the relationship between ritual and social justice."

Now, one might argue that it was the manner in which the sacrifices were offered that upset the prophets. This is not the case. The idea of sacrificing certain animals and saying certain words came directly from their exodus experience. What was missing went beyond the method of sacrifice; it was the lack of concern for the health and welfare of God's people. Even though many were fully aware of the covenant agreement, they still thought that God would not mind their lack of concern for justice, provided that some sort of ritual purity was followed to the temple.

The prophets saw through this and were again incensed! They believed it was like trying to pull a veil over God's eyes. They were fully aware that many would go through the outward gestures of prayer, fasting, penance, and faithful attendance at the temple, but would still refuse to do the will of God when it came to justice. After a while, a number of the Israelites began going though the motions more for show than for anything else—so that others would see how "holy" they were. Jesus would echo this in his introduction to the "Lord's Prayer" (cf. Matthew 6:9–13). They didn't even seem to realize the discrepancy between what they were saying and what they were doing.

Isaiah has a passage where the people speak to God. They ask why they should continue to fast when it seems that God doesn't hear their petitions. They complain that they mortify their bodies, make their beds on sack cloth and ashes, and still God doesn't seem to heed their cries. God's response is to challenge them on what it is that he, the Lord, requires as a fast. His words are clear and to the point:

> "Behold in the day of your fast, your own will is found, and you exact payment from all your debtors. Behold you fast for debates and strife, and strike with your fist wickedly. Do not fast as you have done until this day, to make your voice be heard on high. Is this such a fast as I have chosen? Is not this rather the fast that I have chosen—loose the bands of wickedness, undo the bundles that oppress, let them that are broken go free, and break every burden? Share your bread with the hungry, and bring the needy and the homeless into your house; clothe and cover the naked one, and don't despise your own relatives." (Isaiah 58:3c–5a, 6–7)

In these verses Isaiah challenges all those who would use religion and ritual for their own purposes rather than for serving God. The people wonder why their fasting and prayers go unanswered. Isaiah tells them that their priorities are all wrong. What God expects ritual and fasting to accomplish is entirely different from what the people hope they will bring. God wants worship that manifests itself through justice; the people want worship that allows them to pray and fast without justice. But the prophets would say again and again, "You can not substitute ritual for justice."

It is important to examine more of these verses in Isaiah as they provide good examples of what many prophets do in their writings. Isaiah tells of the importance of keeping the laws of justice as well as the dangers of forgoing justice. First he lays down the law—he tells it like it is, so to speak, "This is what the LORD demands!"

Then he immediately follows up with a promise of hope and good things to come. First you must do justice; you must undo injustice and oppression. Then once you stop fighting God's will, wonderful events will begin to unfold. Isaiah continues his text with these words:

> "Then shall your light break forth as the morning, and your health shall improve, and your justice shall go before your face, and the glory of the LORD shall gather you up. Then if you call, the LORD will hear; if you cry to him, he will say, 'Here I am.'" (Isaiah 58:8–9)

After telling them why their prayers and fasting are not being heeded, Isaiah tells the people that feeding the hungry and clothing the naked are what God requires. He then continues, if that is done God will not only be there for them, but they will be transformed by their own goodness. "Your own righteousness shall be your vanguard."

Isaiah says not only that justice is one of God's demands, but if you treat people justly, the benefits of a just society will be yours as well. However, the central issue is still the doing of justice and Isaiah immediately returns to it.

> "If you will end injustice, and cease to point fingers and make false charges, if you will feed the hungry, and satisfy the needs of the afflicted ones, then shall your light rise up in darkness, and your darkness will be as bright as the noonday. And the LORD will give you guidance and will fill your soul with

brightness, and give you strength; you will be like a well-watered garden, and like a fountain of water whose waters shall not fail." (Isaiah 58:9–11)

We hear the prophet saying that simply going through the motions of prayer is absolutely useless in God's sight, whereas honest attempts to live a life of justice can do wonders for everyone involved.

Without Justice, Empty Prayers

Another interesting point the prophets realized was how phony and mechanical worship can become when one's heart is not in the right place. They knew that anyone could repeat prayers and imitate gestures. Memorizing laws and scriptural verses did not mean (to the prophets) that the laws of verses were firmly implanted in one's heart. The difference between memorizing the word of God and living the word of God can be as different as night and day. Justice towards one's brother and sister is the real manifestation of living God's word; quoting chapter and verse is merely a skill that only requires a good memory. It is one's actions that tell if the word of God has truly taken hold. Without the actions, what you have are people about which the Lord (through Isaiah) says:

> "And the Lord said: For much as these people draw near me with their mouths, and honor me with their lips, but their hearts are far from me; their beliefs are of the commandments and doctrines of men, simply memorized." (Isaiah 29:13)

Jeremiah draws a picture of an Israel, which by this time had become so corrupt and so filled with injustice and oppression that it seemed as if the whole city of Jerusalem was perverted.

> "Go about through the streets of Jerusalem, and see, consider, and seek in the wide places, if you can find any man that acts justly, and seeks the truth, and I will be merciful to that city." (Jeremiah 5:1)

And yet people continued to fill the temple and say their prayers. They ran to the temple with great confidence saying, "This is the house of the LORD." Jeremiah spoke to the men of the temple and shook them up quite a bit by telling them that they were not safe, even in the temple of God, as long as they were involved in oppression. He warned them that they might even be in greater danger there because God might actually destroy the temple rather than have it blasphemed by prayer-quoting hypocrites.

> "Hear you the word of the LORD, all you men of Judah that enter in at these gates to adore the LORD, says the LORD of hosts, the God of Israel: Mend your ways and your doings and I will dwell with you in this place. Don't trust lying words, saying, 'the temple of the LORD, the temple of the LORD, it is the temple of the LORD.' This is a lie. If you will reform your ways and your doings, you will execute judgment between one another. Don't oppress the stranger, the orphan, and the widow, and don't shed innocent blood in this place; and don't follow strange gods to your own ruin. You steal, you murder . . . then you come and stand before me in this house which bears my name, and have said: 'We are safe,' safe you think because you have done all these abominations. Is this house then, which bears my name . . . a den of robbers?" (Jeremiah 7:2b–6, 9a, 10–11a)

Jeremiah dramatically illustrates the same points many of his contemporaries stressed; the absurdity of believing that going to worship could somehow act as a substitute for doing justice. He knew that there were people sitting in the temple who absolutely hated certain others because of their background or family heritage. He also knew that there were people who did nothing—absolutely nothing—for the poor and the hungry living in Jerusalem. He knew there were shopkeepers who paid their workers slave wages, as well as some that treated the powerless in society with utter contempt. He knew that sitting in the congregation there were some that were very violent and cruel, as well as some that were involved in all sorts of crimes. Jeremiah knew all this was occurring. Yet week after week these same people would all come to the temple, ready to go through their religious exercises while in their hearts there was never any real thought of change. Worship became a sort of paying of dues; the people believed it was a way of appeasing God. It became a way of telling God that they would give what they thought was due, while continuing to live selfishly without worrying about the needs of their brothers or sisters.

The prophets repeatedly pointed out that justice and righteousness are the very essence of God. They knew that insofar as worship helped one to know God better and thus his will to see justice reign throughout the land, then prayer and sacrifice were good. But when worship and sacrifice began to take the place of justice, they became unholy in God's sight. If you are not sure what to do, what to sacrifice, what to bring to the house of the Lord, then treat your brothers and sisters fairly and justly, and you will be doing the will of God.

> "What shall I offer to the LORD that is worthy? How shall I kneel before the high God? Shall I bring offerings or year-old calves? Will the LORD be pleased with thousands of rams, or with streams of oil? Shall I give my eldest son for my wickedness, my offspring for the sin of my soul? I will show you, O man, what is good, and what the LORD requires of you—to do justice, and to love mercy, and to walk humbly with your God." (Micah 6:6–8)

Justice and the "One Who Is to Come"

As a point of interest to Christians, we might examine some of the passages which either point to the coming of a holy one (or "servant of God") or which speak about the coming of the new Jerusalem, so we can see the role justice plays in these verses. Isaiah writes some incredibly beautiful and poignant passages about this "servant of God." Whether or not he is indeed writing about the coming of Jesus is not the focal point of this chapter. Rather, the point is that to the Christian world, many of these passages have become associated with Jesus of Nazareth and the kingdom of God. Throughout these passages, the theme of justice ranks high.

> "Behold my servant, whom I will uphold: my chosen in whom my soul delights. I have given my spirit upon him, and he shall bring forth justice to all nations. He shall not cry out, neither shall his voice be heard abroad. The bruised reed he shall not break and the smoking wick he shall not extinguish; he shall bring forth justice and truth. He shall not be sad, or troublesome, until he sets justice on the earth, while islands shall wait for his law." (Isaiah 42:1–4)

Through this powerful imagery, the servant of God, the one personally chosen by God, and with whom he is well pleased, is chosen for a purpose. And that purpose is clear—he will "bring justice to all nations;" he will "set justice on the earth." Whether Isaiah is speaking about an individual or the nation of Israel (scholars generally tend to disagree on this point), the idea is still quite clear. This servant of God would be the one who would live and preach justice to all the peoples of the earth. In fact, the strongest evidence of the servant's authenticity would be his stand on justice. When we get into the New Testament, we will meet a skeptical John the Baptist, asking that

Jesus send proof that he is the one about whom Isaiah spoke. Jesus tells John's disciples, "Go and tell John what you see and hear..." (Matthew 11:4)

A "Righteous Purpose"

According to Isaiah, the LORD calls this servant for a reason, a mission, and a righteous purpose.

> "I, the LORD have called you in justice and taken you by the hand; I formed you, and have given you for a covenant of the people, for a light to the Gentiles; to open the eyes of the blind, to bring the prisoner out of prison, and freedom to those that sit in dungeons in the prison." (Isaiah 42:6–7)

Even without the use of the actual word, we can see how the theme of justice runs through the passage. Note that in the mind of the prophet, justice is associated with freedom. It is not a justice designed to throw people into prisons and dungeons, it is a justice designed to bring people out. But not prisons made of steel and concrete, but prisons of hatred, intolerance, and ignorance. God's justice opens the eyes of the blind, frees the captives, and brings light into the darkness.

Another passage from Isaiah that has also become closely linked with the coming of Jesus (although for many, it is perhaps more known through Handel's *Messiah* than through Scripture) is the one about the birth of the new king. See how in describing his attributes, the motif of justice again plays a prominent role:

> "For a child is born to us, a son is given to us, and the government is on his shoulder; and his name shall be called, Wonderful, Counselor, God-the-Mighty, the Father of the world to come, the Prince of Peace. His dominion shall be multiplied and there shall be endless peace; he shall sit on the throne of David, and over his kingdom; to establish it and strengthen it with judgment and with justice; henceforth, now and for evermore." (Isaiah 9:6–7)

Again you have a description of the actions that will be taken by the person or nation claiming a particular closeness with God. How will you recognize this holy one? What will he do? How will you tell this is the one who is to come? You will be able to know him because justice will somehow touch the land. Those who have always been treated unjustly will suddenly have a new champion. Justice will overturn oppression. Justice will make visible those who have been lost. The proof of closeness to God will be found in the just actions of the servant of God.

Another perfect example of this idea is Isaiah's announcement of the appearance of the Davidic King. Note his description and the actions he will take which will make him recognizable as one truly of God:

> "And there shall come forth a rod out of the root of Jesse and a flower shall rise up out of his root. And the spirit of the LORD shall rest on him; the spirit of wisdom and of understanding; the spirit of counsel and of fortitude; the spirit of knowledge and of godliness. He shall be filled with the spirit of the fear of the LORD and shall not judge according to what he sees, nor decide by what he hears. He shall judge the poor with justice and shall fairly defend the humble of the earth. His mouth will be a rod to strike down the evildoer and with the breath of his lips he shall slay the wicked. And justice shall be the belt around this waist and faith the girdle of his body. The wolf shall live with the lamb, and the leopard shall lie down with the goat; the calf and the lion shall grow together, and a little child shall lead them." (Isaiah 11:1–6)

Here Isaiah speaks about a king who is robed in justice and whose actions are those of one who knows the importance of justice to the God of the covenant agreement. Once more he speaks of the power that justice can have upon the earth, as opposed to the destructive influence that injustice can have if allowed to exist and flourish. If justice prevails, if people are indeed judged not by hearsay or by outer trappings as Dr. Martin Luther King, Jr. would one day say, but by the "content of their character," then real peace can exist on the earth. Justice needs to replace injustice because injustice breeds fear, ignorance, poverty, hunger, and all things contrary to the unifying love of God.

But if through the power of the new king, justice could "roll down like a mighty river," as the prophet Amos suggested, division could be erased, nation could live with nation, and even traditional enemies (such as the wolf and the sheep) could live together. If justice rather than injustice could prevail, much could occur. This was a very important concept of the Old Testament scripture writers—justice as well as injustice plays a profound role in the fabric of the community.

If people are treated unjustly, the consequence will always have a negative impact on the community as a whole. If members of the human family treat each other with contempt or with intolerance, the negative impact will not only affect the oppressed, but the aggressor as well. Parenthetically, the same is true when justice and mercy occur. Justice and charity not only have a positive impact on the poor but on the whole society.

As the prophets understood it, injustice prevents the blessings of God from coming to full fruition, thus causing dissention and strife among all creatures of God. Justice allows the binding power of love to unite all things, even the lamb and the lion, symbols of "natural enemies." However, callousness toward the poor and antagonism toward the least powerful in society will eventually exact a price, paid by all.

In the Book of the Prophet Jeremiah, God speaks to a country on the very brink of disaster. Israel is crumbling from within and about to be overtaken from without. And yet God almost wistfully says that even now things can be changed. He admonishes that this (almost) fallen land could still rise and even be the envy of other countries, if only justice would be lived and trust in the Lord's ways be practiced. If only justice would prevail, a seemingly impossible miracle could occur.

> "If you will return, O Israel, if you will but return to me, says the LORD: if you will take your idols out of my sight, and stray no more. And you will swear, as the LORD lives, in truth, and in judgement, and in justice, and the nations shall pray to be blessed like you, and will praise him." (Jeremiah 4:1–2)

Jeremiah says that even though Israel has moved so far from the community that was once ruled by justice and compassion for the poor, a conversion back to the ways of God could still save the land on the very eve of destruction. But any true repentance must include justice and righteousness towards the needy.

The Spirit of the Lord Is upon Me

Of all the passages in Isaiah that refer to the "one who is to come," or the "servant of the Lord," perhaps chapter 61 is the one most closely identified with Jesus. Jesus cited this passage to announce his ministry to the people of his hometown (cf. Luke 4:18–19). Isaiah 61 is once again an announcement of the purpose of his mission:

> "The spirit of the Lord GOD is upon me, because the LORD
> has anointed me; he has sent me to preach to the meek, to heal
> the contrite of heart, to preach liberty to captives, and release
> to all that are imprisoned; to proclaim the acceptable year of
> the LORD." (Isaiah 61:1–2)

Isaiah certainly recognized the responsibility that went along with being close to the God of love and justice. In Isaiah's mind the new servant of God would be sent to all those in need of God's justice and liberation. The new servant would be sent to all who were poor, victims of oppression or injustice, and indeed the broken-hearted.

How else could the servant of God act but as a liberator? He had to remain faithful to his God whose entire history stressed love and justice. Isaiah believed that anyone claiming to be a "son of God" or a great and holy prophet would have to be this kind of light unto the nations, a deliverer of the poor and oppressed.

Yet simply talking about justice would not prove his "kingship" or "messiahship;" he would have to seek and therefore do justice. Isaiah felt that the future hope was closely linked with the past promise. The new servant of the Lord would be the one who remembered the covenant agreement. He would never forget that God reached down and lifted his people from an oppressive society where their rights had been violated, where their hopes and dreams had been dashed. He would never forget God's desire that the poor and powerless come to know that the very God of creation heard their cry, that they were indeed his people. The new servant would bring hope to replace despair, would give freedom instead of captivity, and would bear light to replace darkness—and would bring:

> " . . . comfort to all that mourn . . . and to give them crowns
> in place of ashes, the oil of joy instead of mourning, a garment
> of praise for the spirit of grief . . ." (Isaiah 61:2b–3a)

In essence, to paraphrase what Isaiah tells the people of Israel, "You have forgotten your promise to God and as a result, you now live in sin. But there is one who is coming who will bring you back to your beginnings. And once again, the loving justice of God will make its way, first to the poor and the exploited, and then to all, and you will remember again the covenant agreement." Is it any wonder that so many people waited in joyful hope for the coming of the Messiah?

Isaiah: A Prophet Who Connects the Old with the New

Here is a final note about the writings of Isaiah pertaining to the one who would be known as the new servant of God. It is important to remember that Isaiah was an Old Testament prophet, as were Micah, Jeremiah, and Amos. Therefore his understanding of justice was that of one compelled to speak out boldly against social iniquity. What differentiates Isaiah from other prophets was that, whereas he castigated his contemporaries regarding their lack of justice, he also spoke of a future hope, of one who would remember the covenant agreement made between God and his people. Thus Isaiah becomes the link between the Old Testament and the New Testament. This becomes a significant point when we get into the ministry of Jesus of Nazareth and what he and others believed his mission to be.

Jesus, the Poor, and the Oppressed

If the prophets were correct, then the Messiah would have a profound effect on the lives of the oppressed and those to whom justice was most often denied. There was a messenger coming with Good News for all of society's outcasts: the poor, the hungry, the powerless, the shunned, those who were sick, those who were considered unclean or possessed, and the "sinners."

As Luke begins, we hear a "voice crying in the wilderness" (Luke 3:4) that one is coming who will bring deliverance. In announcing the coming of the Messiah, John the Baptist also warns the crowds that justice must still be the order of the day.

John the Baptist, sounding remarkably like an Old Testament prophet, cautions the people that they cannot depend on some sort of "special relationship with God" as a way of avoiding the issues of justice and poverty. Jeremiah had given much the same message to the people in the temple (Jeremiah 7:3–12). Like Jeremiah, John the Baptist knew that throughout time people had believed that because of their race or heritage or particular relationship they believed they had with God they might be excused from observing the very essence of God's word: to love, to take care of, and to cease oppressing the poor.

John the Baptist, the last prophet to announce the imminent presence of the deliverer, admonishes the crowds that they had better 'get their act together.' He tells them that all those things behind which people had traditionally hidden would not fool the coming messenger. Only by doing what God had commanded would those who had in some way "made it" in society, make it with the Messiah.

> "Bring forth fruits worthy of penance and do not begin to say, 'We have Abraham for our father.' I say to you, that God is able to make children of Abraham of these stones. For now the

axe is laid to the root of the trees. Every tree that doesn't bear good fruit shall be cut down and burned. And the people asked him, 'What then shall we do?' And he answered them, 'the person that has two coats must share with those who have none, and all who have food must do the same.'" (Luke 3:8–11)

Sharing your possessions and feeding the hungry are both are manifestations of justice as the Old Testament prophets had come to understand it. John the Baptist (or at any rate, Luke) points once again, as did the Old Testament prophets, to the bottom line. Who you are, where you come from, or how close you think you are to God, means precious little if injustice and oppression are a part of your daily lifestyle. So even before Luke reports Jesus saying a word for himself, he reiterates lest anyone forget the importance of simple, basic, human justice to the God of Abraham, Moses, and to Jesus himself.

"And Jesus returned in the power of the Spirit into Galilee, and the fame of him went out through the whole country." (Luke 4:14)

According to Luke, Jesus begins his public life by stating his ministerial mission. He tells the people in his hometown that he is the one about whom Isaiah spoke. He even uses Isaiah's own words to describe his ministry. Luke begins his narrative with Jesus returning to Nazareth and going into the synagogue. He stands up to read from the Scriptures and is handed the scroll of the prophet Isaiah. He opened the scroll and found the passage which says:

"And the book of Isaiah the prophet was delivered to him. And as he opened the book, he found the place where it was written, 'The Spirit of the Lord is upon me. He has anointed me to preach the Gospel to the poor, he has sent me to heal the contrite of heart, to preach deliverance to prisoners, sight to the blind, to give freedom to broken victims, to preach the acceptable year of the Lord, and the day of reward.' And when he had closed the book, he returned it to the minister, and sat down. And the eyes of all in the synagogue were on him. And he began to say to them, 'This day has fulfilled this Scripture in your hearing.'" (Luke 4:17–21)

It is essential to recognize the importance of Jesus' use of Isaiah's words to describe his mission. As pointed out earlier, the prophets constantly reminded people of the covenant agreement between themselves and the God who had entered into their struggle from oppression. What God demanded in return was that justice—that is, an end to oppression and social injustice—the code by which true believers live. Isaiah, who spoke with great passion about the poor, the oppressed, the outcast, the widows, and orphans, also spoke at great length about the one who would bring justice and good news to the oppressed. Jesus recognized the passion of the prophets and by using Isaiah's own words aligns himself with their struggle and cry for justice.

Jesus not only agrees with the prophet's passion for justice, but says that he is the very one who will bring that justice and good news to those who are oppressed. To Luke, this is so significant that he places this passage in the very beginning of his account of Jesus' ministry.

Matthew and Mark both relate this further on in their narratives—Matthew 13:54–58 and Mark 6:1–6. This unbroken line of thinking is expressed from the Old Testament straight through to the New Testament. If Jesus had come preaching salvation without social justice, no one would have believed him. If Jesus had preached a fierce love of God but showed only a general concern about injustice, he would have been received as, at best, just another preacher or prophet. But Jesus immediately identified himself with the poor of society and from his very beginning takes up their struggle. These, after all, were the ones who had been anxiously awaiting him and were in need of the Good News.

Tell John What You See and Hear

Matthew and Luke both tell the story of John the Baptist posing a straightforward question to Jesus, "Are you the one who is to come?" This discourse is a significant and telling insight into the importance Jesus placed on his relationship with the poor and the oppressed—and his acceptance of the role of the "servant" (of which Isaiah had spoken).

John the Baptist, who at this point is in prison, sends some of his followers to ask Jesus if he is the one they have awaited or if they should look for another. Even though, by this point in the scriptural narrative, John the Baptist had already met Jesus and even baptized him, John is simply not sure. He is actually saying, "Tell me the truth; give it to me straight. Are you the one about whom the prophets spoke? Are you the deliverer, the one who will save the poor from oppression and injustice?" Perhaps John had reasoned that his own time was about to end. Maybe John needed assurance that, before he died, God had granted him a look at the one so many had waited for so long.

According to Scripture, John the Baptist's messengers go looking for Jesus and find him among the sick, the poor, and the outcast. They put the question right to him without fanfare, "Are you the one?"

Jesus' response seems to be just as straightforward:

> "Go and tell John what you have heard and you have seen: the blind see, the lame walk, the lepers are cleansed, the deaf hear, the dead are raised to life, and the poor are having the Gospel preached to them." (Matthew 11:4b–5; see Luke 7:22–23)

Jesus tells John's disciples that he is right where Isaiah had said he would be: with the poor, the sick, and the outcasts of society, and that he is doing something about their suffering. It is important to note that neither Matthew nor Luke have Jesus telling John's disciples to go back and recount what he is saying or preaching. Rather, according to Scripture, he tells John to see where he is and what he is doing and decide for himself. Jesus does not ask John to listen to his theology; he tells him to witness his theology. Jesus doesn't ask John to come to a decision based on a new idea; he counts on John's own knowledge of the covenant experience and the subsequent history of the prophets' teachings. Jesus is aware that John knew the Scriptures, as did most good Jews, and that a simple "yes" or "no" answer would not suffice. Instead, he tells John to look at his behavior and then make up his own mind.

It would seem that Jesus wanted to impress John with his (Jesus') personal conviction that actions constituted proof, whereas words alone meant very little. Jesus emphasized that knowing the law and doing the law had to work in conjunction in order to establish the true oneness with the God of Abraham. Simply knowing that justice is important to God is no proof of your willingness to truly follow.

Jesus stressed that not only must you know the importance of justice, but then you must do justice. Not only must you know the importance of feeding the poor, but then you must do something about feeding the poor. Not only must you care about the sick, but then you must do something to help the sick and the suffering.

So, we do not find simply an intellectual discourse taking place between John's disciples and Jesus. We see Jesus laying down a fundamental principle as proof of his closeness to God. Jesus never says that they should tell John only what Jesus was saying; he says, "Tell John what you hear and see."

We see that quoting Scripture alone means nothing to Jesus; instead, knowledge and action are the grounds on which one should be judged. Certainly this view is shared and expressed by many of the prophets; in the New Testament James' letter on faith and good works (James 2:14–26) is firm and clear on the subject also.

On one of the first occasions when Jesus is challenged by someone who sincerely wants to know the plain truth, he places emphasis on his actions—his doing justice among the poor, the sick, and the suffering.

Who Were the Poor?

Who were the poor, the sick, and the suffering? Who were the people with whom Jesus aligned himself? Jesus could be found with those to whom justice was most likely denied. Jesus spent most of his time with those frowned upon by society, the ones whom the "religious people" or the "saved ones" shunned. They were the oppressed, the needy, and outcasts, the people who were blamed for their own illnesses—because of their "sins" or status in society. Just as Isaiah had commanded, Jesus had come to champion the downtrodden. Albert Nolan writes,

> "The people to whom Jesus turned his attention are referred to in the gospels by a variety of terms: the poor, the blind, the lame, the crippled, the lepers, the hungry, the miserable (those who weep), sinners, prostitutes, tax collectors, demoniacs (those possessed by unclean spirits), the persecuted, the downtrodden, the captives, all who labor and are overburdened, the rabble who know nothing of the law, the crowds, the little ones, the least, the last, and the babes or lost sheep of the house of Israel. The reference here is to a well-defined and unmistakable section of the population. Jesus generally refers to them as the poor or the little ones... Today some might refer to this section of the population as the lower classes; others would call them the oppressed." (*Jesus Before Christianity* [Maryknoll, NY: Orbis Books, 1978] p. 21)

From this description we can see that Jesus did not come to comfort only the sick and shut-ins but also those who were considered the dregs of society—those who were "unclean," "ignorant," or "inferior." The poor are not just those who have little money, but also those who have little power, little prestige, and little solace. Joachim Jeremias writes:

> ". . . we can now say that Jesus' following consisted predominately of the disreputable, the *amme ha-'ares*, the uneducated, the ignorant, whose *religious ignorance* and moral behavior stood in the way of their access to salvation, according to the convictions of time.

> But along side this there is a quite different perspective. If we look at the same people through the eyes of Jesus, they appear in another light. He calls them 'the poor,' those who 'labor and are heavy laden.'(cf. Matthew 11:28)" (*New Testament Theology* [New York: Charles Scribner & Sons, 1971] p. 112)

Two points are impressive in both of these descriptions of the poor. The first is the contrast between the way Jesus sees the poor and oppressed and the way the "religious establishment" and the upper-middle class, and the rich see them. To Jesus they are victims; they are the ones who are used and abused by an uncaring society. They are the ones who are helpless and in need of the healing message of salvation. Thus they are also most ready to open their ears and hearts as they recognize their powerlessness and are fully open to the power of God. To many of the rich, the priests, the lawyers, the judges, and those who would point a moralizing finger, the poor are but dirt and rabble. Others in society might consider them with a little less disdain, but still see them as beneath the "upper class." The poor are the ones who are always around begging or looking unsightly—a drain on society. If the message of Jesus was going to change the structure of things in society, the middle and upper class might not be ready to listen and to take heed, for they were, after all, comfortable with things the way they were. Perhaps things weren't perfect for them, but they considered themselves fortunate and favored simply because they were not poor.

The second quality that impresses us in these and other descriptions of the poor in ancient Palestine is their absolute powerlessness during the time Jesus lived on earth. It was believed that everything bad that happened in one's life was a direct result of some sin. It was thought that God was punishing the person because of some infraction, either a personal infraction or one committed by a family member—even as many as five or ten generations back. People also thought they were susceptible to all sorts of "evil spirits" that could attack at any moment. A man would be looked upon as a sinner if born crippled (or because of any number of physical disorders). If he was born into poverty, it could be as "punishment" for something about which he had no idea. Even the disciples held these misguided beliefs. Upon seeing a man born blind,

> "And his disciples asked him, 'Rabbi, who has sinned, this man or his parents, and why was he born blind?'" (John 9:2)

The reverse of this was also held as true. If misfortune was the result of some sin, then good fortune could be the result of "holiness" or some blessing by God. This was an especially popular notion with the elite, the men of the temple, and middle class society members. Many of them viewed their favorable positions as God's sign of their goodness or cleanliness. As a result many felt they had no moral obligation (except, perhaps, a marginal one) to the poor and the powerless. They felt positions were predetermined, so the powerless were made to feel totally abandoned both by society and by God. Nolan writes:

> "It was a dark and fearful world in which the helpless individual was threatened from all sides by hostile spirits and equally hostile men. They were at the mercy of evil spirits who might at any moment inflict them with sickness or madness; just as they were at the mercy of the kings and tetrarchs who possessed them like property that could be acquired, used or disposed of as the politics of the moment required...The poor and the oppressed were at the mercy of the Scribes who loaded legal burdens upon them and never lifted a finger to relieve them. (Luke 11:46) They were denied their civil rights." (Nolan, p. 26)

Nolan ends this striking picture of the poor to whom Jesus came with Good News with his summation:

"Such was the world of the 'downtrodden,' the 'persecuted' and the 'captive' (cf. Luke 4:18; Matthew 5:10). Today they would be called the oppressed, the 'marginals' or the wretched of the earth—the people who don't count. But they were the overwhelming majority of the population in Palestine—the crowds of multitudes of the gospels." (Nolan, p. 26)

We can once again see a clear line of thought running through the Old Testament and New Testament. Micah, Amos, Isaiah, and Jeremiah all passionately spoke against the societal oppression of the poor and powerless that caused the suffering Jesus finds in the people to whom he will ultimately minister. It becomes clear that by the time of Jesus the idea of the covenant agreement, in which all who believed in the God of the exodus experience would do all they could to insure that their society would be free from hunger and oppression, is now but a memory. One would be hard-pressed to look at ancient Palestine and, seeing how the majority of the people lived, know that their God was a God of justice and of freedom. Jesus becomes the specially anointed one who is going to take up the holy cause of the prophets.

Injustice prevails; justice is lost. People are living in darkness—held captive by unjust laws and evil doers. By going to the poor and oppressed, Jesus takes on the role and the responsibility of the servant as defined by Isaiah. In Jesus, the servant takes on human form, human shape, and rises up to do the will and justice of God. As the New Testament writers saw it, now it is Jesus to whom God says:

> "I, the LORD have called you in justice and taken you by the hand; I formed you, and have given you for a covenant of the people, for a light to the Gentiles; to open the eyes of the blind, to bring the prisoner out of prison, and freedom to those that sit in dungeons in the prison." (Isaiah 42:6–7)

In a land of injustice it is Jesus who, by choosing to minister to the poor and the oppressed, becomes God's servant:

> "Behold my servant, whom I will uphold: my chosen in whom my soul delights. I have given my spirit upon him, and he shall bring forth justice to all nations. He shall not cry out,

neither shall his voice be heard abroad. The bruised reed he shall not break and the smoking wick he shall not extinguish; he shall bring forth justice and truth. He shall not be sad, or troublesome, until he sets justice on the earth, while islands shall wait for his law." (Isaiah 42:1–4)

As a result things will be turned upside-down, inside-out, and:

"Every valley shall be exalted, and every mountain and hill shall be made low, and the crooked shall become straight, and the rough ways plain. And the glory of the LORD shall be revealed . . ." (Isaiah 40:4–5a)

The Stage Is Set

From the beginning we see the writers of Scripture recording the account of Jesus' ministerial inauguration in such a way that his vision of that ministry, particularly as it relates to the covenant agreement, becomes clear. Jesus, according to Luke, uses Isaiah's own words to announce the launching of his public ministry. He challenges John the Baptist to use his own knowledge of the Scriptures as a way of proving the authenticity of his ministry. And he chooses to go to the poor and the oppressed of society to bring them the startling "Good News!"

God without Justice: The Hypocrisy Motif

If justice and mercy are keys to belief in the God of Israel, then exhibiting anything short of these, while still proclaiming a deep sense of commitment to this same God, was deemed in Scripture as hypocritical. And if there was any one person despised by the writers of Scripture, it was the hypocrite.

Hypocrisy absolutely incensed the prophets and the other writers because it reduced the image of God from that of a great, powerful, yet loving Father, who cared deeply for all his children, to that of a God who cared more about ritual than human suffering, and more about law than about life. To be witness to hunger, bigotry, and oppression and to do little or nothing about these conditions while still yelling "Lord, this" and "Lord, that" was considered despicable by Jesus and the other great persons of the Bible.

The quintessential ingredient of the exodus experience and the ensuing covenant was God's concern for justice and mercy. Therefore, if social injustice was allowed to exist and oppression allowed to flourish, then what Jesus considered the "weightier demands of the law" were not being met. How one dressed or from where one's family came meant precious little, compared to whether or not one helped ensure that all might live free from injustice.

Jesus levels his most scathing attacks on the Scribes (lawyers) and Pharisees (religious leaders), not because they were villains but because they were hypocrites. They had become men who would hold others to the letter of the law and yet they refused to live by the essence of the law. Some of his most powerful and angry words in Scripture are leveled at the Scribes and Pharisees for many of the same reasons Isaiah, Jeremiah, and Amos were so angry with their contemporaries. Justice is of the utmost concern to God, and where there is poverty, oppression, and hatred, there is seldom justice. In Matthew we see Jesus fuming over the sanctimoniousness of the Pharisees who have placed ritual and tradition above the needs of the poor and the oppressed:

> "Woe to you lawyers and Pharisees, hypocrites! You pay tithes
> with mint, anise, and cumin, and have overlooked the weight-
> ier things of the law; judgment, mercy, and faith. It is these
> things you should have done, and not leave those undone.
> Blind guides! You strain out a gnat, and yet swallow a camel.
> Woe to you lawyers and Pharisees, hypocrites! You clean the
> outside of the cup and of the dish, but you are full of robbery
> and self-indulgence. Blind Pharisee, first you should clean the
> inside of the cup and the dish, and then the outside will
> become clean as well." (Matthew 23:23–26)

Jesus continues his attack on the Pharisees by smashing through the age-
old argument of the hypocrite. The argument that says, "If I had lived back
then, I would have acted differently."

He also goes right to the core—the sad fact that it is easier to hold ceremonies and build monuments dedicated to people of justice and peace than
it is to live as they lived. This, too, is hypocrisy:

> "Woe to you lawyers and Pharisees, you hypocrites! You build
> graves of the prophets and adorn the monuments of the saints,
> and say, 'if we had been alive in the days of our fathers, we
> would not have taken part in killing the prophets.' Admit that
> you are the sons of the ones that killed the prophets. Finish off
> what your fathers began." (Matthew 23:29–32)

Jesus ends his fierce remarks by cursing, swearing (at least in biblical
terms), and foretelling that the Scribes and Pharisees would continue to be
hypocrites and that hypocrisy would continue to exist long after he was put
to death. He also seems to be suggesting that hypocritical religious leaders
and government officials will continue to put men and women of justice and
peace to death, often in the name of religion and order.

> "You serpents, you generation of vipers, how will you flee
> from the judgment of hell? Therefore, I send to you prophets,
> wise men, and Scribes, and some of them you will put to death
> and crucify. And some you will flog in your synagogues and
> persecute from city to city. On you will come all the innocent
> blood of the just that has been shed on the earth, from the

blood of innocent Abel, and the blood of Zechariah, the son of Berachiah, whom you killed between the temple and the sanctuary. Amen, I say to you, this generation will have upon its shoulders the guilt of all." (Matthew 23:33–36)

Justice versus Law and Tradition

What is very interesting about the New Testament sections which deal with hypocrisy is that most of the charges stem from service to those in need as opposed to adherence to the law and tradition. Consider the story about the crippled woman that Jesus healed in the synagogue. The president of the synagogue and its members grew angry over the fact that Jesus had relieved her suffering on the Sabbath. Jesus calls the congregation hypocrites, saying that they treat their animals better than they treat some of their own brothers and sisters:

> "And the Lord answered him saying, 'You hypocrites, does not every one of you, on the Sabbath, release your ox or your ass from the stall and lead them to water? And shouldn't this woman, a daughter of Abraham, that Satan has held prisoner for eighteen years, be released from her bondage on the Sabbath?'" (Luke 13:15–16)

Jesus also spoke out against service in contrast to mere adherence when the Pharisees tried to trap him because his disciples were entering the synagogue without going through the traditional ritual washings. Jesus charged them with breaking God's commandments for the sake of their tradition. He reminded them of the commandment to "Honor (take care of) their father and mother," and pointed out that if it comes to a choice between honoring one's parents or giving to the temple, according to their tradition, the son is obliged to give to the temple:

> "But you say: if a person says to his father or mother, 'The gift from me which benefited you is set apart for God,' then he must not honor his father or his mother. You have voided the commandment of God for your tradition, you hypocrites! Isaiah accurately prophesied, 'This people pays me lip service with their mouths, but their hearts are far from me. They worship me in vain, teaching only doctrines and commandments of men.'" (Matthew 15:5–9)

Jesus also seems angered by those who cast false judgments and accusations. The "holier-than-thou" attitude of so many of the Pharisees, Scribes, and other "religious" people made them look down on others. Because they believed themselves to be saved, the upper class of Jewish society considered the poor and the sinner to be rabble and unworthy. In the Sermon on the Mount (in the book of Matthew), Jesus reminded the people of the prophets' law, which again is the essence of justice:

> "Treat others in the same manner as you want them to treat you, this is the law and the prophets." (Matthew 7:12)

Jesus cautioned all not to be so ready to judge others, no matter who they were or what their position in society. He again pointed to the hypocrisy of those who would sit in judgment of their less fortunate neighbors, especially those not considered "holy:"

> "Any why do you see the speck that is in your brother's eye while you fail to see the beam that is in your own eye? You hypocrite! First you should remove the beam from your own eye and then your sight will be clearer, that you may remove the speck from your brother's eye." (Matthew 7:3–5)

Throughout Scripture we find that Jesus was capable of forgiving anything and yet, for him, the most appalling wrong was hypocrisy. Jesus used his strongest language with religious leaders of the day because they did little or nothing to help the poor and oppressed. The priests, the lawyers, and the authority figures not only refused to be part of the solution, they were actively part of the problem. We see two major sins here. First, nothing was being done for the poor and oppressed of society, and that "nothing" was done in the name of God—who from the beginning, according to all the great prophets, exuded love, justice, and mercy. Second, those who should have been the most prominent in the fight against injustice were often the very ones preventing justice (whether by deed or by consent) from taking place in a society where it was sorely needed.

The New Testament is filled with cases where Jesus held up for ridicule the people who were supposed to be the respected ones of society, both civic and church leaders, because of their lack of concern for the poor and the needy. The account of the Good Samaritan (Luke 10:30–38) and the stories regarding doing good for others on the Sabbath all pointed to the hypocrisy of those who cared little for the poor, all the while claiming a self-righteousness that left little room for true self-examination and an honest change of heart. Jesus knew that all people possess the ability to change, but only after they realize that change was needed. The kind of sanctimonious self-righteousness afflicting the chief priests and lawyers prevented them from seeing their errors.

Perhaps one of the most biting, hard-hitting parables Jesus told to the elders was the parable about the two sons who were asked by their father to do a certain job (Matthew 21:28). Jesus pointed out that the first son, although he said *yes*, did nothing; whereas the other son, who initially said *no*, later changed his mind and did indeed fulfill his father's request. Jesus asked the priests which son had truly pleased the father. "Obviously, the second one," they replied. Without hesitation Jesus stated to the chief priest, the holiest of men in the temple:

> " . . . Amen I say to you, the tax collectors and the prostitutes will go into the kingdom of God ahead of you." (Matthew 21:31b)

It is important to stress here that Jesus was both a faithful Jew and a member of the temple. He was not speaking to members of another religion but to his own religion's chief priests, members of his own faith. They, like Jesus, professed a common belief in the God of Abraham, the Law of Moses and the words of the prophets. And yet Jesus turned to these, the clergy of his church, and told them that tax collectors, men who were considered traitors, and prostitutes would make their way into the kingdom of God before them, the men who knew the Law. That was some indictment! To the Jews, Jesus included, the temple was the holiest place in all the land—so holy that when the temple was destroyed in the Northern Kingdom, it signaled the destruction of Israel itself. And here Jesus was denouncing the men who personified this holiest of places. It would be like a Roman Catholic going to Rome and standing before the pope and all the bishops, telling them that thieves and hookers would get to heaven before they would. It was that strong of a statement.

What Jesus is saying here, and in all his other challenges and charges of hypocrisy, is that the bottom line remained. As in the time of the prophets, the question of how one treated others remained paramount. It still boiled down to justice. What is the greatest law? Love God; love one another; where there is truly love for one another, injustice becomes intolerable. What must I do? Sell everything and give to the poor, the needy, and the oppressed of society (Luke 18:22). What is the bottom line of the law? It is justice, mercy, and good faith (Matthew 23:23). Because the priests no longer wished to believe that mandate, but instead wished to push dogma and preach the nuances of the law, in Jesus' eyes they became so reprehensible that virtually anyone would enter the kingdom before them.

The God they all worshiped, according to Scripture, was one who required the powerful to "champion the oppressed" (Isaiah 17). But the temple and its clergy were not the champions of the oppressed. Instead, either because of fear, greed or callousness, they became part of the oppressive process that kept people poor.

Kahlil Gibran brings the various personalities of the New Testament to life and has them giving testimony "in their own words" about their life and times with Jesus. It is interesting to read Gibran's perspective of how Jesus viewed hypocrisy as unforgivable. He writes an imaginary conversation between the apostle Luke and Jesus. Luke asks why Jesus is willing to forgive and console all the sick, the weak, and the sinners except for the hypocrite. Jesus answers:

> "You have chosen your words well when you called sinners weak and infirmed. I do forgive them their weakness of body and their infirmity of spirit. For their failings have been laid upon them by their forefathers, or by the greed of their neighbors. But I tolerate not the hypocrite, because he himself lays a yoke upon the guileless and yielding. Weaklings, whom you call sinners, are like the featherless young that fall from the nest. The hypocrite is the vulture waiting upon a rock for the death of the prey." (*Jesus, the Son of Man* [New York: Charles Scribner & Sons, 1971] p. 112)

The Crux of the Problem

It is important to note that the tension between Jesus and the Pharisees, the priests, the lawyers was not caused by their failure to believe that he was who he said he was—even though most did not. Rather, it was that they had inherited a rich tradition of wisdom and knowledge from the prophets that was based on the covenant agreement. It was perfectly clear on the subject of poverty, oppression, racism, and bigotry against aliens and mercy. And yet these men who should have exemplified that tradition failed to live by these principles. For those who studied the law, there could be no escaping the absolute importance social justice played in their relationship with God. But, as Nolan describes, the people of Jesus' time were living in social and economic poverty and oppression that in some ways was as bad as what their ancestors had endured before God delivered them from the Egyptians. It is meaningful here to focus on the words of the prophets. Remember Micah who said:

> "What shall I offer the LORD that is worthy? I will show you what is good, and what the LORD requires of you: to do justice, to love mercy, and to walk humbly with your God." (Micah 6:6a, 8)

Remember the consistency with which God (through) Amos reminds all about the covenant agreement:

> "It was I who brought you out of the land of Egypt . . . Listen to these words, all you Israelites, which the LORD speaks to you, to the whole nation that I brought up from Egypt." (Amos 2:10a, 3:1)

Also remember the prophets' absolute condemnation of oppression and social injustice, either by an individual or by a community:

> "See the great disorders among her the people and the oppression in her midst . . . you who oppress the poor and put down those in need." (Amos 3:9a; 4:1b)

> "Oh, you that upend justice and turn righteousness to the ground. They have hated the one that rebukes the gate, and have despised the one who speaks the truth. And you robbed from the poor . . ." (Amos 5:7, 10–11a)

> "But judgment shall be revealed as water, and justice as a mighty torrent." (Amos 5:23)

Also remember the words of Jeremiah who both warns the house of David and accuses those who have become oppressors:

"Administer justice in the morning, and rescue the one that is oppressed, lest my indignation be like a fire that no one can quench . . ." (Jeremiah 21:12)

"And you will swear, as the LORD lives in truth, in judgment, and in justice . . ." (Jeremiah 4:2a)

"Therefore they grow great, enriched, gross, and fat, and have evil thoughts and have not practiced justice. They haven't corrected the causes of the orphans, the widows, and they haven't provided fair judgment to the poor." (Jeremiah 5:27b–28)

And recall the words of the prophet Isaiah:

"Woe to you who make wicked laws filled with injustice, laws that oppress the poor, do violence to the weakest people . . ." (Isaiah 10:1–2a

"Uphold justice and do what is right . . ." (Isaiah 56:1a)

"Is this not the fast that I have chosen for you, to loose the ropes of wickedness and undo the ties that bind . . . and lift the burdens of the oppressed?" (Isaiah 58:6)

"For I am the LORD that loves right doing and hates injustice and robbery." (Isaiah 61:8)

The list goes on and on, but what is essential to remember here is that these are the prophets that the Scribes and Pharisees claimed to believe and held as examples of the way their faith in God should manifest itself. Yet they were pursuing the lighter matters of the law while living a good life and doing little or nothing to help the poor and oppressed.

As mentioned earlier, if Jesus was going to claim to be the one about whom Isaiah had spoken, then justice and righteousness had to be among his chief concerns. Since the Pharisees neither pushed for social justice nor tried to overthrow the kinds of oppression that gripped so many of the multitudes, this was a key element in the eventual and inevitable breakdown between the religious establishment and Jesus. He called them hypocrites and liars because, although well versed in the law, they did little to help the needy. Isaiah foretold that justice would be at the very foundation of the one who was to come, but the Pharisees proved to be as unjust as the Roman occupiers. When justice (in the form of Jesus) met injustice, a clash was inevitable.

The Pharisees felt that simply "keeping the law" made them holy and just. Jesus told them that because they didn't actively work for the poor and the oppressed (and indeed were oppressors themselves), their fasts and rituals didn't matter. They were snakes and vipers—hypocrites that broke the real law of God.

It seems that as much as the priests and lawyers disliked the Romans who were occupying their land, they were not willing to have their position as men of God challenged. The more Jesus preached the truth of justice and righteousness, the more the Pharisees saw the very essence of their own religion turned against them. At the same time that the Pharisees were quite outraged that a pagan Roman army had dared to oppress the chosen people of God, Jesus came along and challenged them on their own oppression of the chosen people of God. Whereas the Pharisees attempted to use the law and the writings of the prophets to point an accusing finger at the Roman occupiers, Jesus used these same laws and writings to call the Pharisees oppressors—and to do so publicly, in front of the Israelites and the Romans.

Jesus accused the Pharisees and Scribes of being worse than those of the occupying Roman Empire because they professed to believe in a God of freedom and justice; while the Romans professed no such belief. Jesus pointed out their hypocrisy, both to the crowds and to the Pharisees themselves. They could ill afford to have their own hypocrisy thrown in their faces again and again. The Pharisees and the chief priests were left with only two real choices: they could either repent, or they could eliminate Jesus. Again Kahlil Gibran records their decision eloquently through the character of Luke:

> "Then the hypocrites of the land laid hands upon him and they judged him; and in so doing, they deemed themselves justified. For they cited the Law of Moses in the Sanhedrin in witness and evidence against him. And they who break the law at the rise of every dawn and break it again at sunset, brought about his death." (*Jesus, the Son of Man*, p. 112)

The Good News

Two attributes come to mind when one examines the Good News. The first is the tremendously freeing effect it had on those who, because of ignorance and oppression, were held captive. It freed them because the most popular belief of the time led the poor to believe that their misery, their poverty, and their oppression were all due to their own sin. Not only did the state treat them miserably, but the religious leaders led them to believe that God was treating them miserably as well. These people were often burdened by social and economic conditions as well as with guilt because they believed that they were without hope and that it was due to their own fault. The poor had no prestige, no recognition in society; even God did not seem to honor them in any way. Without God's love and thus his protection, they were left vulnerable to become "captives of Satan" (Matthew) and could spend their whole lives diseased and impoverished. Perhaps the greatest link in the chain of captivity around the neck of the poor was one that suggested a lack of hope. There was no hope offered to the poor, so like those who are forced to live in a prison without any hope of parole, many lived resigned to a lasting torment.

With the Good News, Jesus absolutely exploded the myths. He completely turned around what the people were thinking and feeling. He told them not only that God cared about those who are poor, but that they were actually special in his eyes. Unlike other men of religion, Jesus didn't tell them they had to change before he would associate with them. Instead, he mingled with them, ate with them, and slept in their houses. Both by works and by deeds he said to the poor, the outcast, and those oppressed by the official religious leaders—that God loved them, just as they were, and waited with open arms for them, his children. Again, whether or not one wishes to argue that Jesus was accepted as the Messiah or Son of God is not the issue. What was important was that Jesus was accepted by many as a great prophet and holy man—if nothing else—and this very holy man, unlike the Pharisees or Scribes, would not only associate with the poor and the oppressed but would also touch them, spend time in their company, and tell them the wonderful Good News that they were indeed blessed in the eyes of God. One can only imagine the effects this must have had on those who had been held prisoners of the belief that they were hated, even by God, with little hope of ever being anything of worth.

When one considers, in the light of today's knowledge, the connection between the psychological and the physical aspects of human behavior, one can readily see what effect being touched by a "representative of God" had—thereby freed from a sin or a sentence that was thought immutable—on an individual. It is not my contention to minimize the miracles of Jesus as being psychosomatic in nature. Also I do not wish to dismiss the devastating effect emotional or psychosomatic illnesses can have on a person. I believe that for many, just being told—perhaps for the first time in their lives—that they were loved by God and forgiven of their sins would be enough to have an incredible healing effect on both mind and body. For the first time, some had faith in themselves because they believed through Jesus that God had faith in them. Thus their poverty, sickness, or hunger didn't keep them from God. Instead, they were told that they were close to God because of the suffering placed upon them by others. The poor would surely consider this sort of news to be wonderful and good.

The second striking point about the Good News is that Jesus clearly asserts that God is also quite concerned about the physical sufferings of the poor. This is a major point to be considered, particularly if one has been victimized by oppression. Jesus demanded not only concern for the poor but also an elimination of the attitudes that cause poverty, as well as an alleviation of the miseries surrounding the oppression of the poor. The poor and oppressed were suddenly told (actually reminded) that God is concerned with people getting not only spiritual comfort, but actual physical comfort as well. I think this was of great significance in the impression Jesus made on the poor and needy. Jesus showed the God of Israel as being concerned with whether or not they were lonely, cold, or hungry at night; not as the austere, stern God of ethereal principles that the Pharisees and Scribes often tried to make him to be. According to Jesus not only did God care, but he cared greatly. In fact, if these basic needs were being denied to any of his people, then mere knowledge of law, ritual, and tradition would mean nothing when judgment came.

The Sheep and the Goats

> "And when the Son of Man comes in majesty and all the
> angels with him, then shall he sit on the throne of his majesty.
> And all nations shall be gathered together before him."
> (Matthew 25:31–32a)

If there is any doubt about the idea of God's concern for the basic needs of life for the poor, the 25th chapter of Matthew sets the record straight. The parable of the sheep and the goats speaks more bluntly about this topic than any of the others. The Great King will come to judge the nations. He will separate everyone into two groups, the sheep and the goats. His criteria will be neither knowledge of the law (in the sense of being able to recite what is written), nor adherence to fasting practices, nor positions in society (priest, official, etc,). There will be only one basis for judgment: adherence to the principles of justice as found in the Scripture.

- Did you do anything about the suffering of the poor?
- Did you feed the hungry?
- Did you do anything for all the poor who were without clothes or shelter?
- Did you do anything for those who were made to feel like strangers or aliens or made to feel just plain different? Did you welcome them into your homes?
- Did you do anything for those who were locked away, whether in actual jails or in prisons of fear and bigotry? Did you reach out to them?

> "Then shall the king say to everyone on his right hand,
> 'Come, you blessed of my Father, possess the kingdom pre-
> pared for you from the foundation of the world. For when I
> was hungry, you gave me to eat; when I was thirsty, you gave
> me drink; I was a stranger and you took me in; when I was
> naked, you covered me; and when I was sick, you visited me.
> I was a prisoner and you came to me.'" (Matthew 25:34–36)

As in so many of what I've come to call "the bottom line Scriptures," what is essential here is the understanding that one of the most important aspects of fellowship with God is reaching out to those who are victims of an oppressive society. According to Matthew, upholding basic human rights is one of the keys to salvation. God separates the "sheep" from the "goats" not based on their religious affiliations, but on their efforts to ensure freedom from hunger, fear, imprisonment, illness, and alienation. The question of allegiances would come centuries later in the writings of the early church.

Note the element of surprise in the voices of the sheep. Some of them show astonishment that suggests them saying. "You saved us? Why? We were never members of your sect or affiliated with your group."

> "Lord, when did we see you hungry, and feed you, or thirsty and give you drink? And when did we see you a stranger and took you in, or naked and covered you? When did we see your sick or in prison, and come to visit you?" (Matthew 37–39)

The king answers and tells them why they were chosen. They ask in astonishment, "When?" The king answers that because they did this for the poor, the outcast, and the needy, because they cared and gave of their time and resources that they were saved. It was also because the Great King could be found living not in the palaces or the temples of the rich and powerful, but among the very people that they shunned—and he, in fact, was one of them. Therefore what was done to one of these, the poor and oppressed, was done to him:

> "And the king answering, said to them, 'Amen I say to you, as long as you did it to one of these, my least brethren, you did it to me.'" (Matthew 25:40)

There is, of course, another side to this parable, the side of the "goats." They, too, are rather surprised with their fate. I believe their surprise is due to the fact that they had done the things they believed were the proper and respectable things to do. I would guess that when they found out that they were not exactly in the Great King's favor, their opening statements of protest would include mention of what they felt was a clean record, which should have spoken for itself. They probably would complain of unfairness, citing their attendance records at the temple, their belief in the God of Israel, their support of their leaders, and perhaps even their faithfulness to their spouses. Surely they would have objected to the idea that they had denied a Great King anything as basic as food or clothing:

"'Lord, when did we see you hungry, or thirsty, or a stranger, or naked, or sick, or in prison, and did not minister to you?' Then he answered them saying, 'Amen I say to you, as long as you did not do to the least, neither did you do it to me.'" (Matthew 25:44–45)

I believe, therefore, that the Good News to the poor and oppressed people of ancient Palestine was that God was (and would continue to be) squarely on their side. Jesus tells the poor and oppressed that in a special way they become God's people. He emphasized once again, as always, that God hears the cries of his people and is not only moved to compassion but also is moved to action. God becomes so closely involved with his people that he actually becomes one of them. Thus Jesus warns the powerful that now when they work to oppress the poor, God Almighty is taking it very personally because he is also being oppressed. Once again you can imagine the impact this news must have had on the poor. In their eyes God was no longer against them, as some had led them to believe; God was on their side. No wonder the poor loved this prophet and man of God.

It is also no wonder that the established rulers had Christ killed. The Good News, after all, stood in direct contrast to everything that the established religions and their leaders taught. The idea that God called to himself those that the Pharisees labeled "rabble" and "immoral" instead of them, the duly appointed leaders of the faith, was more than their pride could stand. Joachim Jeremias writes:

"The world among Jesus based man's relationship with God on his moral conduct. Because the Gospel did not do that, it shook religion to its foundation. Thus the stumbling block arose from the Good News—and not primarily from Jesus' call to repentance." (*New Testament Theology* [New York: Charles Scribner & Sons, 1971] p. 119)

Jesus and the Outcast

Jesus and Zacchaeus

Perhaps no parable than that of Zacchaeus shows the depth of Jesus' commitment to change people by love rather than by punitive measures. In order to understand the power of Jesus' actions in this parable, one has to understand the relationship between the Jewish people and tax collectors. As mentioned elsewhere in this volume, tax collectors were seen as traitors. This was the perspective because of their willingness to make their living serving Rome, at the time an occupying force in Israel. It is rare in any culture that one deemed to be a traitor garners much sympathy. Many of these tax collectors became very wealthy and that wealth must have been as a slap in the face to the poor living under the oppression of Rome. So when Jesus talks about tax collectors, he is talking about a group generally hated by most.

According to the parable recorded in Luke 19:2–10, there lived a chief tax collector, Zacchaeus. When he hears that Jesus is coming to his village, he climbs a tree so he can see him. Why did he climb a tree? The most popular answer has always been because he was a small man and could not see over the crowd. However, one would think that if he was a man of influence and respectability, he could have simply pushed his way though the crowd to get a better look. Undoubtedly he would have gotten a better glimpse of Jesus by standing in front of the crowd (rather than looking down from a tree limb). It's my hunch that he was at the back of the crowd for two reasons. One, he felt unwanted in the midst of his own people. He had probably accepted his lot as an outsider, loved by neither Romans nor his own people, and knew he would not be welcomed in the crowd. My second reason is because it was probably not very safe for him to go into such a large crowd who had such strong feelings about his profession. Being a man of small stature, pushing his way through such a potentially hostile crowd could have cost him his life.

So Zacchaeus chooses to make his way up a tree and watch the proceedings from a distance. But Jesus notices him and somehow sizes up the situation and makes an absolutely startling pronouncement. Christ says to Zacchaeus:

> ". . . he (Christ) looked up and said to him, 'Zacchaeus, come down right now as I must stay at your house.' Zacchaeus came down at once and greeted him gladness." (Luke 19:5–6)

The people respond with outrage, although the Scripture passage makes it seem somewhat milder than it probably was. We are told:

> "When the people in the crowd saw what Christ did, they began to talk among themselves, saying, "He has chosen the home of sinner as a place to stay."" (Luke 19:7)

The obvious observation clearly suggests that the people were upset that Jesus would go to the house of one of the towns most disliked citizens. However, I believe what transpires here goes much deeper than this simple idea of Jesus visiting the home of a tax collector. We are dealing with the culture of a people. If Jesus went into the home of this man, some important cultural things transpire. Once Jesus had entered, the tax collector would offer him something to eat, or at least to drink. It would have been the height of disrespect to invite someone into your home and not to offer them some water, food, or wine. But in that Middle Eastern culture, sharing in a meal has tremendous significance—it is a powerful cultural sign that bonds people together. If you were estranged from one another, sharing in a meal meant you were once again in union with your neighbor. It further meant that what ever went on before, no matter how negative, must now be put behind you. Sharing a meal meant that you were no longer enemies, but friends. That was the power in that culture of sharing a meal. It was somewhat like the sacred tradition of sharing a peace pipe among Native Americans. To share in that act meant an end to hostilities and the joining together of people who may have been enemies. It is why the Samaritan woman was surprised that Jesus (the Jew) would want to drink water from her well. Even sharing a drink from the same well had significance to the people of the region. It is also why many of the Pharisees complained of Jesus' behavior earlier on in the Gospel of Luke when he chose to eat with sinners and tax collectors. This kind of thing was simply outrageous to those who regarded themselves as "good."

> "The tax collectors and sinners were gathering in close to hear him, but the Pharisees and the teachers of holy Law grumbled, 'This man welcomes sinners and eats with them.'" (Luke 15:1–2)

As products of our contemporary society, we might miss the significance of mentioning *eating*, regardless of the fact that Jesus was *associating* with sinners. At the time this was written, scripture writers wanted to leave no doubt about exactly what Jesus was doing with these sinners. Jesus was not just visiting with these people, which to some may have been outrageous enough! But Christ was communing with these sinners—an act which many considered to be the ultimate betrayal.

The people were outraged since they would be clueless as to what this traitorous tax collector could have possibly done to merit such forgiveness. He hadn't renounced his profession. He clearly had not been sufficiently punished for his crimes against his own people. Even if he had renounced his dreaded profession, surely there should have been some punishment that he should have suffered for all of the misery caused. Furthermore, as a tax collector, he grew rich while serving their oppressor. How could Jesus go to his house and embrace him as a brother? This was probably why the people were angered by Jesus' seemingly simple act of inviting himself to the house of the tax collector.

The more one studies Jesus, the more one notices that Christ rarely passes up an opportunity to teach the will of his Father to people in very practical ways. Jesus believes that love is stronger than all else. In the case of Zacchaeus, he teaches the people the power of unconditional love. Rather than demand a pound of flesh from the tax collector, Jesus instead embraces him as a brother, as a son of God and a child of Israel—no matter what his sinful nature has made him. And Jesus was no fan of tax collectors. He often used the term to deride those he wished to criticize. When he leveled his harshest criticism at the Pharisees, he compared them to tax collectors. Yet when he meets this real life tax collector, rather then shun him as would have been expected, he chooses this man's house above all others as a place to rest, eat, and make a friend of the town's enemy.

Once again Jesus draws a sharp distinction between the ways of the world, and the ways of his Father. He uses the opportunity to show publicly that the world's solutions are not always what work in the Kingdom of God. Jesus must have thought he'd found an ideal subject to whom he'd display God's unconditional loving justice—this little man up in a tree!

The most startling aspect of this particular parable is Zacchaeus' response to Jesus' unconditional love and mercy. We are not privileged to the substance of the conversation inside Zacchaeus' house, but we do know of the outcome of Jesus' visit. Zacchaeus was completely transformed by the experience and he began to act in ways unlike a typical tax collector. I believe Zacchaeus' transformation is the central theme of this parable. Zacchaeus was changed—not by the people and their methods of persuasion and intimidation—but by Jesus' unconventional approach. One again Christ rejects an eye for an eye, and instead turns the other cheek, taking the chance that Zacchaeus might reject his offering of love. Jesus embraces the child of God within, reaching beyond the surface and calls Zacchaeus to a place of light, a place of goodness that the people did not often see (and even Zacchaeus may have forgotten). The Lord doesn't offer damnation—he offers love—and the results are remarkable.

> "Zacchaeus said to Christ, 'Look, Lord. I'll give to the poor half of my possessions. If I have cheated anybody of anything, I'll pay back four times the amount.'" (Luke 19:8)

What Jesus is interested in is results, a transformation to take place, and repentance to happen. By reaching into this man's heart with love, he changes him forever, and at the same time keeping him alive. What many of the people wanted was justice—but not in the way we have come to understand biblical justice. They wanted justice in the way the world has come to understand it. Many people were justifiably upset with this man's behavior as they may have been personally cheated (or even ruined) by this greedy tax collector. They wanted more from him than what could pay for his crimes. If one examines this story more closely, you can see that the people got something more than temporary vengeance, they got something practical. Those who were cheated suddenly found themselves in possession of twice what they'd lost. Who in the crowd criticizing Jesus' approach to Zacchaeus would have ever dreamed that Christ's methods would have produced such a result?

Jesus and Levi

> "After this transpired, Jesus went out and saw Levi, a tax collec- tor, at his place in the tax booth. Christ addressed Levi saying, 'Follow me.' Levi arose, leaving everything behind, and fol- lowed the Lord. Then Levi prepared his house and staged a great meal for Jesus. A large group of tax collectors and others also ate with them. But the Pharisees and the teachers of the holy Law complained to his disciples, 'Why do you sit at table, eating and drinking with tax collectors and sinners?' Jesus answered them, 'The healthy are not in need a doctor, but the sick are. I have not come to implore the righteous, but sinners to repentance.'" (Luke 5:27–32)

In the same way Jesus calls another tax collector, Levi and tells him to follow him. Imagine the shock and surprise Levi must have experienced, following Jesus only to end up at his own home. While Scripture doesn't go into detail, one could imagine that Levi thought he was going to be lectured—perhaps at the gates of the temple—or maybe humiliated in the village square. But instead, Jesus once again takes the dreaded tax collector to Levi's own home. Surely he was going to eat and drink with this man who was hated by the people.

Scripture points out again the practicality of Jesus' methods. First he distances himself from the self-righteous who can not see beyond their own traditions. Again, just as with Zacchaeus, there are people questioning the method Jesus uses in dealing with "a sinner." And even though it seems clear that the people have had no effect on Levi, they persist, regardless of the results. Once again it is obvious that Jesus is interested in results. He breaks the well-established taboos because he is more interested in saving Levi than he is in punishing him—so Christ goes to Levi's home.

I find it most interesting that Scripture tells us that Christ not only ate in Levi's home, but that Levi actually threw a big party in honor of his guest. Additionally, Scripture records that many tax collectors came to the party. It is clear that Levi, the sinner, knew other sinners—people just like him—to invite to his party. Here Jesus is given the opportunity (while at table) to teach many people in need of hearing the Good News. If Jesus had simply shunned Levi, he may have never gotten the chance to minister—to not only Levi—but to his many friends as well. Because Jesus didn't have a self-righteous attitude when he approached sinners, they felt more at ease with him, thereby opening themselves to his mercy and his goodness. Many of the so-called "righteous" projected a haughtiness that kept them separate, and they rarely had the opportunity to minister to these people so in need of God's loving mercy.

Jesus and Matthew

Interestingly, this story appears to be almost an exact duplicate of Levi's story. Jesus once again calls someone, not to the synagogue but to that person's own home. Again he eats with him, and again others of Matthew's persuasion come and join them. This gives Jesus the chance to minister to a whole group of sinners rather than just one.

> "Jesus went out from there and saw a man named Matthew sitting in the tax collector's booth. Christ said to him, 'Follow me.' Matthew got up and followed Jesus." (Matthew 9:9)

The Kingdom of God

One cannot help but be struck by the marked reversal of values in the Kingdom of God versus the kingdoms of the earth. Who are the people who traditionally have had access to a king and who usually possess the power to influence in an earthly kingdom? Most often it is the people with wealth, education, prestige, and authority. Those who have the least influence are the poor and the outcast. In fact, the poor are often victimized by the very people who rule the kingdoms of the earth. The values at work here are money, power, prestige, and human values; yet true moral values, such as justice and equality, are often looked upon as secondary (I'm being generous). How one looks, what one wears, with whom one associates, and—in particular during the time of Jesus—what and with whom one eats are highly significant to one's position in the kingdoms of the earth.

The Kingdom of God as proclaimed by Jesus, however, is totally the opposite. The Kingdom of God is a kingdom of justice; it is a place where looks, wealth, and education mean little. What is important is the way one's brothers and sisters are treated. And so the poorest, most unattractive, uneducated prostitute who supports her younger brothers and sisters with the money she earns enters the gates of the justice kingdom before the educated, honored priest who doesn't do anything for the poor or the needy. The tax collector who admits he is a sinner gets preferential treatment over the eloquent lawyer who recites all the prayers of the Torah self-righteously. The hungry, the needy, and most of all, the powerless in earthly societies are the very ones who are given the places of honor in the justice kingdom.

Everything about the Kingdom of God is contradictory to the way any natural, "self-respecting" kingdom operates. In the Kingdom of God, love is more important than honor and justice is more important than prestige. During biblical times both Rome and the kingdom of the Jews must have stood in stark contrast to this Kingdom of God about which both John the

Baptist and Jesus preached. Yet it is to this Kingdom of God that Jesus called the people—this kingdom of his and not the one of the world.

One must also understand the concept of kingdom in all of its political light. Established kingdoms were very much in place during the time of Jesus. Between Rome and the Jewish people there already existed an emperor, numerous kings, princes, governors, senators, church leaders, generals, and government officials. Two working political kingdoms complete with laws and institutions were in place, but they operated like most earthly kingdoms, perpetuating the dominion by the rich and the powerful. Like other worldly kingdoms, they had an insatiable appetite for glory, power, land, and riches. Human values and rights were always seen as secondary to the greater honor and glory of the state or the empire. The temple eventually bought into the idea that the whole was more important than any one group or individual (John 11:50). Rather than challenging empires or kingdoms where justice was denied, the religious officials thought that perhaps it was better to try to live under the dominion of Rome than to oppose it and possibly become much like the poor, oppressed victims themselves.

Jesus clearly and precisely challenged the earthly kingdom and all of its representatives because it intruded into the laws of the greater kingdom, the Kingdom of God. By preaching to the poor and oppressed in the manner in which he did, Jesus was saying to all that the powerful kingdom, which in many ways actively kept the poor in need and the hungry without food, was not the last word in kingdoms. He was proclaiming an even greater kingdom, ruled by an even greater king. And he advised all that they should first seek to comply with this greater kingdom's values and with this greater king's justice. He also warned the "powerful of earth" that the Kingdom of God was dawning and there was virtually nothing they could do to stop it—yet another slap in the face of the authorities!

Jesus assessed that the kingdom present during his time was contrary to the Kingdom of God in that it did not promote God's justice as he had manifested it throughout the ages. Therefore, the present kingdom was extremely flawed. Again, it is important to point out that many of the poor saw the kingdom (the Roman government) working together with the temple leaders to bleed them dry, both with burdensome laws and with outrageous taxation. Just as God was all-powerful in their eyes, so too must the Roman Empire have seemed omnipotent. This must have produced an atmosphere of extreme hopelessness for the poor. Jesus not only openly criticized the kingdom of the land but also suggested to the poor that those responsible for their oppression would be judged quite harshly in the greater Kingdom of God. Luke's version of the Beatitudes is very strong on this point. Here Jesus tells the poor, the hungry, and the hated that they should not despair because in the really great kingdom they, the cursed and despised, are blessed.

> "Blessed are you poor, for yours is the kingdom of God. Blessed are you that hunger, for you shall be filled. Blessed are you that weep now, you shall laugh. Blessed are you when men hate you and when they shall separate you and insult you, and cast out your name as evil, for the Son of man's sake. Be glad in that day and rejoice; for your reward is great in heaven, in the same way did their fathers treat the prophets." (Luke 6:20–23)

Then Jesus also warned the rich, the well fed, and those who were overjoyed with their own success that they should beware. He stated that they would have to pay for their callousness when the kingdom that was already dawning would arrive:

> "But woe to you that are rich, for you have had your consolation. Woe to you that are well fed, for you shall hunger. Woe to you that now laugh, for you shall mourn and weep. Woe to you when all bless you; just so did their fathers treat the false prophets." (Luke 6:24–26)

Jesus must have seemed like a true champion of the oppressed—as Isaiah had described the coming servant—not only because he was he willing to stand up for them when he spoke to them in private, but he was also willing to state aloud what was in many of their hearts. The poor must have been very impressed with his bravery, if nothing else. After all, who were the rich? Who were the well fed? Who were most likely to scoff at the poor? It would probably have been the governors, the senators, the generals, the temple officials, and all the successful businessmen—all the power brokers of the present kingdom. They were also those who stood to lose the most if a new kingdom replaced the old one and those who were most in the position to harm Jesus.

It is important to remember that Jesus was tried and convicted of treason. He was put on trial and executed for suggesting that no king and no state had the right to create a climate that proved contradictory to the values of the Kingdom of God, and that no kingdom—intentionally or not, could set itself up as the Kingdom of God. Jesus was killed and much of the early church was persecuted for pointing out to the nations that no matter how powerful the kings or kingdoms became or how much loyalty to the state might be demanded, those who followed God must first and foremost be loyal to the ethics of the Kingdom of God. According to Jesus, no kingdom was greater than God's Kingdom. Such talk was considered highly political and in fact, treasonous. Capuchin Friar Michael H. Crosby writes:

> "In the face of the link between the economic and political realities that conspired to create enormous wealth by the exploitation of slaves and the poor (cf. Revelation 18:1–8), the early church gave the example to future generations to live by a comparable ethic based on the need to de-legitimize any power or principality that takes to itself the divine prerogatives and interprets itself consciously or unconsciously as the kingdom of God." (*Thy Will Be Done: Praying the Our Father as Subversive Activity* [Maryknoll, NY: Orbis Books, 1977] pp. 61–62)

Although the idea of a Kingdom of God can be found in parts of the Old Testament, certainly the teachings of Jesus brought the concept to greater fruition in the New Testament. The idea of a Kingdom of God coupled with the Good News was enough to make Jesus at once extremely popular among the poor and oppressed—and enough to win him many powerful enemies, as his eventual fate would prove.

> "Your throne, O God, is forever and ever; the scepter of your kingdom is a scepter of justice." (Psalm 45:7)

When trying to understand the Kingdom of God (in contrast with our contemporary society) is the very concept of "kingdoms." As mentioned earlier, during the time of Jesus kingdoms were everywhere and everyone, even the poor and the illiterate knew the basics of how a kingdom worked. And the most basic fact about kingdoms was they were ruled by kings. And kings had absolute power over their subjects. Kings did not rule by public opinion polls, they ruled by divine right. When Jesus spoke of the Kingdom of God, it was understood by all that it would be ruled by a king, God, who would have the ultimate authority over all who would come under its realm.

Therefore, when he proclaimed the dawning of the kingdom, all who would hear knew that the choice was simple; to either accept it in its entirety or to reject it. (Clearly it was a choice not given to them in the earthly realm.) No one could live in a kingdom and have a choice as to which of the king's decrees to accept or reject. This is very important to consider in the modern world. In ancient times, people understood that if the king issued a command that seemed difficult, the biggest problem for the subjects was to try and find out *how* to obey—not *if* to obey. But that kind of thinking has long since been replaced by notions of democracy where everyone feels they have a right to his or her say in matters that affect their lives. But the Kingdom of God is not a democracy. One can either accept the Kingdom of God, or reject the Kingdom of God. What one cannot do is accept the Kingdom of God and then try and run the Kingdom of God. And so, even though there will be a profound shift in the makeup of the body of this kingdom (in contrast to an earthly one), it will still adhere to its basic form in that it is ruled by God, and not by its subjects. That is how people understood governments in antiquity.

What Jesus went about saying was that God had a plan for humans to follow, a way of life that all subjects must live by. He never allows for people to challenge God on the rightness or wrongness of his rule. What he does do is help people learn how to follow what God calls them to do, and gives them the assurance that whatever the king commands will ultimately be right for all who would follow. He tells them that his very presence is the unequivocal sign that the king's love for his people is so great that he has been sent to assure them that this king is good in all things and just to all people. But obedience and faith must come first for all who would be a part of the kingdom. And while Jesus often rejected the title of king himself, he did accept the title of lord. A lord is, after all, part of the hierarchy of a kingdom. But when people rejected his words and his commandments, he questioned them on why they would refer to him as "lord" if they were not willing to obey his commands, just as one would do in any earthly kingdom.

> "And why call you me 'Lord, Lord' and not do the things which I say?" (Luke 6:46)

Perhaps this is why according to Jesus, it was so hard for the rich to ever enter the Kingdom of God. While the poor, as mentioned earlier, knew how to be subservient to a greater power because that situation was forced upon them most of their lives. The rich were used to having at least a certain amount of power within the confines of a kingdom. Even if it was only the illusion of power, the rich knew that they could at least expect a fair hearing on their views because they believed that their wealth entitled them to some consideration. But the poor knew they were often at the mercy of the rich and powerful. Thus the rich, in order to enter the Kingdom of God had to give up more than money; they had to give up the power associated with being rich. They also had to learn the meaning of earthly powerlessness in order to be able to place them under the complete and total authority of the King of Heaven. For some, it was just impossible—even though for some the desire may have been genuinely there. In Mark's Gospel, the rich man is disappointed both with the answer Jesus gives, as well with himself when he asks what he needed to do in order to enter the Kingdom of God. He was concerned since God's realm was everlasting and it might bring him the promise of everlasting life.

> "And when Jesus began on his way, a man ran up and knelt before him. He asked, 'Good Master, what must I do to receive life everlasting?' And Jesus responded, 'Why do you call me good? No one is good but one, that is God. You know the commandments, do not commit adultery, do not kill, do not steal, do not lie, defraud no one, and honor your father and mother.' The man then said to Jesus, 'Master, all these things I have observed since I was young.' And Jesus looked on him lovingly and replied, 'One thing is lacking—go and sell whatever you have and give to the poor, and you shall have treasure in heaven. Then come, follow me.' The man felt sad at that and went away sorrowful as he had many great possessions that were important to him. Jesus looked around and said to his disciples, 'How hard it is for those with riches to enter into the Kingdom of God!'" (Mark 10:17–23)

In the same manner, Jesus also holds up children as examples. They too, much like the poor, are powerless in society. They are totally dependent on their parents for survival. They hold neither wealth nor political power, and much like the poor, they know their lives depend on a power greater than their own. When children came to him, Jesus used them as examples of the type of persons most likely to understand and thus enter into the Kingdom.

"And they brought infants to Jesus that he might touch them. When the disciples saw this, they rebuked them. But Jesus called the infants to him and said, 'Let the children come to me and do not stop them. Theirs is the Kingdom of God. Amen, I say to you, whoever will not receive the Kingdom of God as a child will not enter it.'" (Luke 18:15–17)

Herein lays the dilemma for our contemporary, democratic society. Accepting the Kingdom of God like children is something foreign to our way of thinking. In today's largely democratic societies, kings are little tolerated. Accepting ideas or commands without questioning them is a concept long since forgotten. America became a country, after all, because we could no longer stand being under the totalitarian rule of the king of England. Yet the Kingdom of God calls all subjects to accept the kingship of God and the lordship of Christ completely. It calls us to give up certain privileges of independence in order to receive far more as a servant, a child, and a citizen of the Kingdom of God. Intellectually most Christians can understand the concept of complete and total surrender to the Kingdom.

In many Protestant churches people are often asked when seeking membership into a congregation if they accept Jesus Christ as their personal Lord and Savior and absolute ruler of their lives. While one would most certainly answer with a resounding "yes," for most it is still (emotionally) a hard pill to swallow. When Jesus gives a command such as "turn the other cheek," too often we want to know the full reason for making (what seems on the surface to be) such an outlandish request. We don't quite get that it's not a request, but a command. If not convinced that the argument for such an idea is noteworthy, we feel we have the right, having been born in a free and democratic society, just to say "no."

Only the poorest of the poor seem able to understand and to follow the concept of total and complete surrender to the authority of the kingdom, having been forced to live without the trappings of earthly power in the kingdoms they toiled in on earth. Perhaps that is why Jesus says in Matthew, "Blessed are the poor in spirit" (Matthew 5:3).

The Good Shepherd

It has often been said that one can never fully appreciate the true depth of the Bible without first understanding something of the history and the period of time in which it was written. Often the tremendous magnitude of some of the messages found in the Bible is reduced to simple stories of right and wrong because we don't understand the nature, customs, and politics of the people to whom they were originally addressed. For instance, one can never fully appreciate the meaning of a term like "the good shepherd," a phrase that seems innocuous enough, until one understands just what kind of job shepherding was in the time of Jesus—and the kinds of profound political ramifications that phrase could have.

Consider that shepherding was often a difficult and dangerous job, particularly if you were a "good" shepherd. The image in the mind moves from one reminiscent of Little Bo Peep to one who works endless hours—often in the bitter cold—fighting off wolves and bandits, while still providing care and protection to the flock.

Even the term "good" can be misleading. Many people might think that Jesus was referring to his nature or perhaps his personal integrity when, in John 10:11 he refers to himself as a "good shepherd." But when one understands the people to whom this was addressed, one can see that it was far more important to speak of "good" in the sense of a job qualification than in terms of some innate personal quality. These simple, nomadic Middle Eastern people knew firsthand what shepherding was all about. Even if many of them were not shepherds themselves, it was such a way of life for this rural people that virtually everyone had an appreciation and understanding of what was meant by the term "good" shepherd. They could empathize because they had to go through many of the same sacrifices every day. They also knew that being the kind of "good" shepherd that John speaks about was more than a job. Shepherds literally had to risk their lives in the mountains and valleys fighting thieves who would steal their sheep or wolves that would kill and eat their lambs. They understood that the difference between a good shepherd and a bad shepherd was often the difference between life and death for the flock.

Certainly every shepherd hearing this story could appreciate the tremendous time-consuming and self-sacrificing commitment necessary when assuming the role of a good shepherd. It took a special kind of love and commitment that went far beyond the duties of a typical employee. They knew that hired help often would not face up to the dangers of the road, preferring to run from the peril rather than risk personal injury:

> "But the hired man, not being a true shepherd and whose sheep are not his own, sees the wolf coming. The man flees and leaves the sheep behind and the wolf catches and scatters the sheep. And the hired man is salaried and has no real care for the sheep." (John 10:23–13)

To the hired help, being a shepherd was just a job, hardly worth getting hurt or even killed over. The good shepherd, however, would risk his own life for that of his flock. This was at once both extraordinary and yet, at the same time, not so extraordinary to the shepherds of ancient Palestine. After all, that was what being a good shepherd was all about. It's like hearing about a mother who risks her life running into a burning building to save her child. It is at once extraordinary and yet not so; after all this is what most good mothers would do if their children were in danger—often without even thinking about it.

To a modern person, particularly an urban one, the whole idea of a good shepherd might simply conjure up some rather romantic or serene picture—complete with images of soft pastoral music, warm sunsets, and gentle breezes. Then Jesus the Good Shepherd appears as the rather soft-spoken, gentle sheepherder who watches over you while you graze quietly in the fields. Phillip Keller, a modern day shepherd in East Africa, states:

> "Many who either read or study the Scriptures in the twentieth century come from an urban manmade environment. City people, especially, are often unfamiliar with such subjects as livestock, crops, land, fruit, or wildlife. They miss much of the truth taught in God's Word because they are not familiar with

such things as sheep, wheat, soil, or grapes." (*A Shepherd Looks at the Good Shepherd and His Sheep* [Grand Rapids: Zondervan, 1977])

The story of the good shepherd takes on a dramatic twist to the people of ancient Palestine or to the people in parts of Africa (where nomadic traditions of shepherding still exist).

It is important to note the tremendous significance of Jesus assuming the role of the good shepherd to those who had been considered the unsaved and the rabble by the religious establishment. To the poor and oppressed, Jesus' offer was remarkable. He was presenting himself as their protector, as one responsible for their lives, their comfort, their health, and their welfare. He was willing to assume the role of arbitrator in their times of dispute. He was willing to be their sacrifice if that was what it took to keep them safe from harm. To the shepherds and other ordinary people of the day, it was an extraordinary invitation for such a holy man to make. For the poor and oppressed it would have been an astonishing revelation.

Let's accept the premise that the majority of the people Jesus spoke with were poor and oppressed, and that they were kept that way by those of the rich and mighty Roman and Jewish establishment. It is then evident how a self-proclaimed representative from God, offering to become a shepherd to the poor, might be regarded as dangerous and unpopular by the religious establishment. After all, if Jesus was claiming to be a good shepherd and the poor and oppressed were to be his flock, then who was to be cast as the thieves or the wolves in this metaphor? Once again it would be the political and religious establishments—the rich and the powerful—all who "lined their pockets" by exploiting the poor and the hungry.

Again, we see the writers of Scripture giving us the classic scriptural confrontation: the rich and the powerful pitted against the poor and the weak. Whenever that confrontation arises in Scripture (or scriptural literature), God takes the side of the poor, the oppressed, the weak, and the powerless. Whether they are seen as the slaves in Exodus, or as the destitute and oppressed in the writings of the prophets, or as the widows and orphans in both the Old and New Testaments, or as the sheep needing protection from the hungry wolf in John and Ezekiel, God is always there in a special way for the poor and the powerless.

Shepherd as a Political, Religious, and Historical Metaphor

There is something else that must be considered in any examination of the good shepherd motif. This is perhaps the most important point: the role the good shepherd played in Jewish religious history. Even though the image of the shepherd is used in Isaiah 40:10–11 and Jeremiah 23:1–6, perhaps the prophet Ezekiel wrote most eloquently on the theme. In Ezekiel 34, his writing about the shepherd is very strong, both in language and imagery, on three points:

- the need for a good shepherd;
- why God was angry with those who were supposed to be "good" shepherds but were not; and
- what made them "bad" shepherds, thus creating the need for a new shepherd to replace them.

In this chapter Ezekiel writes a powerful condemnation of the religious leaders, the "shepherds of Israel," for failing to protect and indeed abusing the poor and oppressed. This is best illustrated when he points an accusing finger at the shepherds who were not doing their job.

"Woe to the shepherds of Israel that feed only themselves. Should not the shepherds feed the flocks? You drink the milk and you clothe yourselves with the wool, and you slaughter the fat animal, but you fail to feed my flock. The weak you have not strengthened, and the sick you failed to heal. You didn't bandage the wounded and you failed to seek the lost of the flock. My sheep were scattered because there was no real shepherd and they became the prey of all the beasts of the field and were scattered. My sheep have wandered on every mountain and on every high hill and my flocks were scattered upon the face of the earth. No one watched after them. Therefore, shepherds, hear the word of the LORD. As I live, says the Lord GOD, my flocks have been made prey to all the beasts of the field because there was no real shepherd. The shepherds did not seek after my flock and they fed themselves instead of my sheep. Therefore, shepherds, hear the word of the LORD, behold I come upon the shepherds, I will take back my flock from them." (Ezekiel 34:2–10b)

Ezekiel's words are full of straightforward, no-nonsense imagery that is hard to misinterpret. He paints a clear picture of the crimes of the "bad" shepherds and in so doing, lays down a job description of a "good" shepherd. He writes about the greed and the total lack of concern these shepherds have for the sheep. He talks about the indifference of the "bad" shepherd towards the hungry, the sick, and the lost. At the same time he points out that they grow rich and powerful over the labors and troubles of the sheep. Then he threatens to remove all those shepherds and replace them with a "good" shepherd:

> "I will release the shepherds from their duties and they will care only for themselves no longer. I will take back my flock from the shepherds so the exploitation my sheep might end." (Ezekiel 34:10b)

Ezekiel confronts those who are supposed to be shepherding with the reality that the poor and oppressed are being neglected. Not only that, but they are being oppressed by the same religious establishment whose job it was to protect them from oppression. Ezekiel points to the greed and callousness of the shepherds, citing that they look only after themselves, often at the expense of the poor and needy:

> "Was it not enough for you to feed on good pastures? Must you also tread your feet on the rest of the pastures? When you drank the clean water, you stirred-up mud in the water with your feet. And my sheep were fed what you had trampled with your feet and they drank the muddy water you stirred-up . . . I will save my flock and it will be not be treated this way anymore." (Ezekiel 34:18–19, 22a)

God's solution to the problem is simple and straightforward. He will simply put in place a shepherd who will do the kind of job he insists on; he will bring forth a good shepherd:

> "And I will appoint a shepherd to watch over them. My servant David will feed them and he will be their shepherd." (Ezekiel 34:23)

What clearly differentiates the good shepherd from the bad one is his willingness to put the welfare of the sheep above his own personal or political conditions. To pretend to be a shepherd while at the same time being indifferent to (or contributing to) the endangerment of the sheep placed in your care made you a cowardly scoundrel, not worth the wages you were paid. By assuming the role of the good shepherd, Jesus not only challenges those in power, but he uses a religious and historical precedent to do so. Certainly, all the Pharisees knew of Ezekiel's writings on the good shepherd. They also would have been very aware of the implications of having someone other than themselves cast as the "good shepherd." They were, in effect, being cast as the shepherds who no longer cared for the sheep, the traditional "bad guys" of the Ezekiel story, and thus they needed to be replaced. For the purpose of this work it is important to stress that the crimes of the shepherds of Ezekiel's time and the crimes of the Pharisees were virtually the same. Both simply did not care enough for the poor, the oppressed, the hungry, and those in need. In one sense, we can see that the writers of Scripture wished to draw a parallel between the problems during Ezekiel's time and those during Jesus' time insofar as the solution—namely, God replacing the bad shepherd with a good shepherd—remained the same for both.

If God Didn't Ordain That We Be Poor, Then Why Are We Poor?

I'm sure there came a point when those in power grew concerned that the poor might start believing that they were so loved by God that he would repeat history and send them a new shepherd. Not only could this action lead to the poor asking some rather embarrassing questions, but it could also mean that the poor would ask these questions under the protection of the shepherd who came from God. Many of the poor, with a new-found sense of security provided by the good shepherd, might find the courage to ask questions such as:

- Why are so many of us poor whereas so many of the priests and scribes are rich?
- If being poor is not a theological issue, why am I forced to live in hunger and in poverty?
- If I am not paying for some sin that either my ancestors or I committed, why am I living in poverty?

Perhaps an even more concise way of stating it might be:

- How come the shepherds are so full whereas we, the sheep, are so hungry?

This could present the Pharisees with a rather delicate dilemma. The Jews were living in an occupied land. Those members of the Jewish establishment who were rich and somewhat powerful were living that way only at the pleasure of the Roman government. The Romans could care less about the Jewish god, prophets, and laws. The only purpose the Jewish religious establishment served for them was to help keep peace among the Jews. Rome was willing to placate the Jews and their religion only because it meant less work and trouble for Rome. However, the religious leaders were supposed to be shepherds for the Jews. They were supposed to protect the sheep from all enemies, but the shepherds sold out in order that they might maintain a better standard of living. With Jesus assuming the shepherd's role, especially in the light of Ezekiel's statements, the whole balance became threatened on two levels. First, as already mentioned, the poor might begin to ask difficult questions about their state in life; second, the existing shepherds would be exposed for what they were and become less useful to a hostile occupying government. Peace would therefore be threatened—even though it was a peace for which many had to pay a high price. Perhaps this was why the Pharisees accused Jesus of (among other things) subversion (cf. Luke 23:2).

Historically the idea of a good shepherd is not meant to imply someone passive or pastoral in the traditional Western sense. It is meant to suggest a tireless fighter for justice and freedom. The shepherd in Scripture is the one who faces down the oppressor and protects the sheep. When David, perhaps the most famous of all the shepherds in Jewish history, volunteered to fight the giant Philistine warrior Goliath, Saul tried to discourage him. David's reply provides insight as to what a good shepherd does, a description that is far from passive:

> "'I am the shepherd of my father's flock; when a lion or a bear is about and carries a sheep away from the flock, I will pursue after them. I attack it and rescue the sheep out of their mouths. They then rise up against me and I catch them by the throat and I strangle and kill them. As the shepherd, I have killed both a lion and a bear: and this uncircumcised Philistine will be as one of them . . . who has dared to curse the army of the living God.' And David said, 'The Lord delivered me from the lion and the bear and he will save me from the hand of this Philistine.'" (1 Samuel 17:34–37a)

David went on to become perhaps the greatest king in Jewish history. Whether the story of David and Goliath is based more on legend than on fact is not so important for this work. What is important is the perception the Jews held of the enormous strength and power given to those who would be their "Father's good shepherd," along with the tremendous courage associated with anyone holding that position. Shepherds who were indeed "good," who cared for their sheep above all else, and who were blessed by God, were seen as giant killers. It is easy to conclude that the "giant" could be a system or an establishment, as well as a Philistine.

Perhaps the greatest lesson the figure of the shepherd is meant to instill is that those who would be shepherds of the Lord must have concern for their flock's poor and oppressed members, and to be there for their problems at all cost! The scripture writers wanted to make clear that without such concern, shepherds were lacking in their duties and therefore need to be replaced. It also seems as though the writers wanted to convey a sense of fearlessness when it came to protecting the sheep from all who would endanger them, no matter who they were or how big their armies. I'm sure this doesn't mean that shepherds never became frightened. Jesus certainly felt alone and scared in the Garden of Gethsemane. But all who would be shepherds of the Lord must be willing to live and die for the welfare of the sheep. To the writers of Scripture, this was after all, what being a "good" shepherd was all about. One can see that this image of the good shepherd is a far cry from the image often depicted on holy cards or portrayed in stained-glass windows.

The Samaritans

Perhaps the greatest testimony against the sin of prejudice and racism is found in the works dealing with the Samaritans. Much like the story of the good shepherd, no one in ancient Palestine would have missed the enormous significance of portraying the Samaritans in any favorable or heroic light to the Jewish people. There existed a long running mistrust (and at times hatred) between the Samaritans and the Jews dating back to the sixth century BC. In order to understand the immensity of this hatred and mistrust, it is necessary to look at the history of these two groups.

Israel had been occupied by a succession of conquering armies beginning with the destruction of the Northern Kingdom by the Assyrians in about 721 BC. The Assyrians were followed by the Babylonians fifty years later, the Persians in the sixth century BC, and then Alexander the Great in the fourth century BC. After the Greeks came the Ptolemies, the Syrians, and by the time of the New Testament, the Romans.

When the Assyrians occupied Israel, they deported many (though not all) of the Jews. At the same time they imported outsiders from Babylon and Mesopotamia to help increase the dwindling population as well as to "resettle" Israel. Eventually those who had been repatriated intermarried with those who had been left behind. The Jews who had been left behind also began to incorporate some of the religious customs and practices of those brought in from the outside. It is this intermarried, bi-religious (though still predominately Jewish in faith) group that would eventually be known as the Samaritans.

Some two centuries later, after the Assyrian occupation, Cyrus, king of Persia, decided to allow the exiled Jews to return to Jerusalem and rebuild their temple. He sent word to Babylon where a rather prosperous colony of Jews had settled, and afforded them the opportunity to return to their homeland. Many Jews accepted Cyrus' offer and returned to Jerusalem under the leadership of Shesbazzar, also known as the ruler or prince of Judah, to begin construction of the new temple. The actual building of the temple was done under the leadership of a man known a Zerubbabel; this will become significant as we go on. When the Babylonian Jews returned to Jerusalem they were met by a people who came from Jewish ancestry like them, but who were now "different" in many ways. It was the coming together of these two groups and their subsequent clashes which would be at the center of centuries filled with hatred and mistrust.

A Problem of Orthodoxy

One of the ties that held the exiled Jews together was their staunch adherence to the writings and teachings of Judaism. During their exile they also adopted many of the teachings of the prophets. Their religion was a way of maintaining an identity in a foreign land. The Judaism that was practiced by those who had remained in Jerusalem, however, was not only fused with Assyrian customs but was also without the works of the prophets. The returning Jews felt that their religion, which to an Israelite was one's whole life, was being debased and diluted. The Samaritans, on the other hand, felt that the returning Jews were being high-handed and self-righteous. However, the Samaritans did try to extend reconciliation to the Jews by offering to help build the temple, but Zerubbabel flatly and harshly turned down this offer:

> "Now the enemies of Judah and Benjamin (Samaritans) heard that the returned children of the captivity were building a temple to the LORD the God of Israel. They came to Zerubbabel and the heads of the families and said to them, 'Let us help you build for we seek God as you do . . .' But Zerubbabel, Jeshua, and the rest of the family heads of Israel said to them, 'You have no need to help us build this house to our God, but we must alone build it to the LORD our God . . .'" (Ezra 4:1–3)

As can well be imagined, this came as a slap in the face by the Jews to the Samaritans and didn't do much to cement good relations between these two related peoples. The Babylonian Jews, and in particular, the Yahwist priesthood, simply felt that the Samaritans were no longer ethnically or theologically pure, and therefore they wanted little to do with them. The

Samaritans were angered by this attitude and tried to plot against the Jews, thus preventing them from building their sacred temple. They wrote to the Persian King Asasuerus (generally believed to be Xerxes, the son of Darius I) and suggested that if the Jews were allowed to build the temple, and more importantly, the walls around the city of Jerusalem, they might be encouraged to become insurgents. Likewise, a letter was addressed to Asasuerus' son, Artaxerxes, when he became king, making these charges:

> "To Artaxerxes the king, from his servants. Be it known to the king that the Jews . . . are in Jerusalem and rebuilding that rebellious and wicked city, setting up the foundations and repairing the walls. Be it known to the king that if this city is built up and the walls are repaired, they will not pay general levy, tolls, or taxes, and these losses will harm the king. But we have eaten salt at the king's table and we count it a crime to see the king wronged. Therefore, we have sent this to inform the king. Search the history books and you will find written accounts in the records stating that is a rebellious city and hurtful to the kings and provinces, and that wars were started here in the past. For these matters the city was destroyed. We testify to the king that if this city is rebuilt and its walls are repaired, you will no longer have possession on this side, west of the Euphrates River." (Ezra 4:11–16)

Even though this letter (written the Samaritans would have one believe, totally out of a sense of patriotic duty towards the monarchy) did manage to postpone the construction of the temple, eventually the temple was built. But this clash between the Samaritans and the Jews laid the groundwork for the hatred and contempt that would continue to exist for centuries. Other situations simply compounded the problem. For instance, the Samaritans, having been rejected by the Jews, built a rival temple on the summit of Mount Gerizim, and this became their main religious center. The Samaritans believed it was on Mount Gerizim that Abraham prepared to sacrifice his son, Isaac; the Jewish priesthood believed that this had taken place on the Temple Mount of Jerusalem. This became still another point of contention. By the time we reach the New Testament writings, the hatred and mistrust between the two groups had grown immeasurably.

It is important to look at this hostility from the Jewish perspective because it was to the Jews that the Samaritan parables were originally addressed. During Jesus' time their animosity had so grown that no Samaritan's testimony could be used as evidence in a Jewish court of law. The Samaritans were publicly cursed in the synagogues and no one was allowed to eat or drink with them. Likewise, Jews were not welcome in Samaritan villages; there were even many reports of Jews being killed in such places. The animosity had developed into blatant bigotry. I believe it is safe to say that hatred for the Samaritans had become (for some) a fundamental part of Jewish culture and religion by the time Jesus began his ministry. It is against this historical backdrop and its accompanying racism that the stories of the Good Samaritan, the ten lepers, and the woman at the well were told. It is important to note that even Jesus' disciples had to grapple with their own prejudice when it came to the Samaritans, as we can see in Luke's writings:

> ". . . they went ahead of him and entered into a city of the Samaritans . . . but they would not receive him because his ultimate destination was Jerusalem. When his disciples, James and John, saw this they said, 'Lord, will you have us call fire down from heaven that the fire may consume them?' He turned and rebuked them . . . and they went to another town." (Luke 9:52–56)

One can see the enmity existing between Jew and Samaritan just by this passage. Jesus had to turn to this own disciples—men who had traveled with him, had heard him speak, and knew his feelings—and rebuke them for their attitude. As far as John and James were concerned, the whole village could go up in flames; they were even willing to pray for that destruction. Perhaps this was all said in moment of anger and the disciples would not really have wished harm on the whole village, but it is most often in moments of such anger that our deep prejudices come to the surface.

There are two important points here. First, this incident in Luke's narrative follows a number of events dealing with justice and love, such as the Sermon on the Mount and the narratives on hypocrisy. Even after hearing all this, the apostles' prejudices are still prevalent enough to come to the surface when provoked. The second point is that this incident about the Samaritan village comes just before the story of the Good Samaritan. Perhaps Jesus, having just gone through this episode with two of his disciples, felt that it was time to address this issue directly. Nevertheless, Luke uses this opportunity in his narrative to tell one of the most famous of Jesus' payables, that of the Good Samaritan.

And Who Is My Neighbor?

> "A man was journeying from Jerusalem to Jericho and was accosted by robbers. They stripped and beat him and left him half-dead. It happened that a priest was traveling down the same road. When he saw the beaten man, he went to the other side of the road and passed on by. Then a Levite came along. He, too, crossed to the other side of the road and walked on by." (Luke 10:30–32)

There are two implications that the people would have noticed immediately in this story. The first is that the priest and the Levite were cold to the plight of the dying person, even though he was one of their own. The second is their willingness once again to put tradition and law above the needs of their brother. At that time it was a traditional belief that coming in contact with a dead body along the road would have rendered them unfit for temple duty. Part of the hesitation of the priest and the Levite would have undoubtedly been based on their reluctance to take the chance that this man might die in their presence. It was simply not worth it to take that risk. However, as Luke illustrates here and in other chapters, Jesus once again puts the health and welfare of the person above tradition of law:

> "But a Samaritan traveler who came to him was moved to pity. He went up and tended to his wounds, pouring oil and wine on them, and then wrapping them in bandages. Then he lifted him onto his own beast and brought him to an inn and watched over him there. On the next day he produced two silver pieces and gave them to the innkeeper, saying, 'Watch over him. If you need to spend more to do this, I will repay you on my way back.' Which of these three, in your opinion, was neighbor to the robbers' victim?" (Luke 10:33–36)

With this parable Jesus not only reiterates the prime law of God, "love God, love your neighbor," but he also uses this opportunity to denounce the prejudice and hatred that had been going on between the two groups for centuries. I'm sure that to many Jews this story was totally unacceptable. All who heard it were being asked to draw the obvious conclusion that all people are neighbors regardless of race or religion. Racism, prejudice, and religious bigotry—all were considered against God's nature and will as far as Luke was concerned, and the Samaritan story was a perfect illustration of these precepts. Jesus could not have picked more apt anti-heroes to bring home his point. Undoubtedly the Samaritans were the brunt of many ethnic slurs, and several people in the crowd would probably have preferred to make the robbers be the heroes and the Samaritan the victim, believing that the only good Samaritan was a dead Samaritan. But Jesus insists it is one's action that determines the goodness of an individual, not a person's race or even religion. Jesus again illustrates this in this story about the ten lepers:

> "As he was entering a village Jesus was met by ten lepers. They stood away from him and called-out saying, 'Jesus, Master! Look on us with pity!' He saw them and said, 'Go and present yourselves to the priests.' And while they were going they were made clean. One of the lepers, upon finding himself cured, turned and glorified God aloud. He threw himself at Jesus' feet and gave him thanks, and he was a Samaritan. Jesus responded, 'Were not ten cured? Where are the rest? Is this foreigner the only one to come back and give praise to God?' Jesus then said, 'Rise up and be on your way; your faith has cured you.'" (Luke 17:12–19)

Once again the hero of the story is the "foreigner," the one who did not belong to the same church or neighborhood as Jesus and the rest of the Jewish community.

The Samaritans as Seen through the Eyes of John

Of the four Gospels, John's is considered the last to have been written. His account is somewhat different from the other three in that John was not only recording historical events but he was also giving definition to much of their content. He was also writing for an already established church. One must remember that by the time of John's writing, seventy to one hundred years had passed since the death of Jesus. In his book John Wijingaards, MHM writes:

"At the time when John's Gospel received its final shape, the other editions by Matthew, Mark, and Luke were already widely used in the Christian communities . . . John's intention was to go farther . . . writing for mature Christians who were already familiar with the truths of the Gospel. John provides a more profound insight into the personality of Christ and the purpose of his life, death, and resurrection." (*Handbook to the Gospels: A Guide to the Gospel Writings and to the Life and Times of Jesus* [Ann Arbor, MI: Servant Books, 1977] p. 65)

This knowledge can be a valuable tool as we study John's use of the Samaritan metaphor. When he tells the story of the Samaritan woman at the well, we are not only getting a valuable parable from Jesus, we are also getting the moral message that John believed the early church should have as members of a movement dedicated to the teachings of Jesus.

The Woman at the Well

John begins his narrative of the woman at the well with Jesus again passing through a Samaritan village. Stopping at a well, he asks a Samaritan woman for a drink:

"A Samaritan woman came to collect water. Jesus said to her, 'Give me a drink.' The woman from Samaria replied, 'What, a Jew asking a drink from me, a woman of Samaria?' Jesus responded to her saying, 'If you only knew what gift God gives and who it is asking you for a drink, you would have asked him and he would have given you living water.'" (John 4:7–10)

Here is yet another reminder of the relationship between Jews and Samaritans. The Samaritan woman registered shock upon hearing Jesus' request and then feigned sarcastic surprise. "You, a Jew, ask a drink of me, a Samaritan woman?" As mentioned earlier, no Jew would ever drink from the same cup as a Samaritan or even drink from the same well. Yet in John's Gospel Jesus is not only willing to share the same cup as the Samaritan woman, but he is also willing to share the Good News or "living water" with her. To modern day Christians this might seem like a nice Christian thing to do. Once again we must realize that for many of those hearing this for the first time, the idea of Jesus even talking to this woman and then offering her this "living water" (even if they weren't sure just what "living water" was) would have been enough for them to dismiss Jesus as a heathen.

An even greater shock would have been the way John deals with the whole question of the temple. As I mentioned earlier, the Jews built their temple in Jerusalem, whereas the Samaritans built their temple on Mount Gerizim. This caused great conflict between the two groups. But again, to the evangelist wishing to teach a theology of Christ, God is greater than temples and sects. John faces the issue squarely:

> "'Sir,' said the woman, 'It's obvious that you are a prophet. Our forebears worshiped on this mountain, but you Jews say that the temple is the place to worship God in Jerusalem.' 'Believe me, woman,' Jesus said to her, 'the time is coming when you will worship the Father neither on this mountain nor in Jerusalem . . . But the time is approaching and is already here, when authentic worshipers will worship the Father in spirit and in truth. These are the worshipers the Father seeks to worship him.'" (John 4:19–24)

I believe that this statement takes on added significance. Jesus is not only involving himself with the Samaritan woman, but he also strikes a blow at the ultraconservative members of the priesthood as well as members of the general Jewish population. They would have considered an issue like the locating of the temple to be sacrosanct. To some members of the community this statement would have been huge! It would have been considered radical, perhaps even subversive. But to Jesus, the welfare of the people and their souls bore more importance than laws and tradition. John does not dismiss the law and tradition. He simply would not hold them above the well-being of the people they were meant to serve. John ends their conversation by saying that God is spirit and those who worship him must worship in spirit and in truth. The issue of where the worship takes place is not what is most important.

In the next verse John, like Luke, is willing to show the misgivings that even Jesus' own disciples had about the Samaritans:

> "At that moment his disciples returned and they were astonished that he was talking to a woman. And yet not one of

them said, 'What are you looking for?' or 'Why are you talking with her?'" (John 4:27)

Even though the passage just says "a woman," it is reasonable to assume that the disciples' uneasiness stemmed from the fact that she was a Samaritan woman. There are plenty of instances in other sections of the Gospels where Jesus spoke freely to women without the disciples feeling such concern.

John's narrative about the Samaritans concludes with Jesus going to a Samaritan village and staying there for two days. Again this is an action of great significance. When one considers that even sharing a glass of water would have caused a great deal of furor in many Jewish circles, staying in a Samaritan town for two days would have been scandalous. It means Jesus would have most likely eaten their food, slept in their beds, and played with their children; all this while preaching that they were all members of the single family of God. In a style typical of the evangelist, he makes the point that many Samaritans believed in Jesus not because of any miracle or magic, but because he was able to rise above traditional rivalries and prejudices and in some way touch their lives:

> "They told her, 'It is no longer because of what you stated that we believe, for we have heard him with our own ears, and we know that this is in truth the Savior of the world.'" (John 4:42)

It is no accident then that the Samaritans were used in Scripture to illustrate actions speaking louder than words. For many, perhaps the hardest thing to accept in the Good Samaritan story is that there is no mention of the Samaritan converting from one religion to another. For all we know, the Good Samaritan remained a Samaritan until the day he died. What was important to Luke was that the Samaritan's actions were such that Jesus could hold him up as an example for all future generations to emulate. Yet for centuries there would be a persistent argument in much of the Christian world over whether one's deeds or good works meant much of anything in comparison to whether one was Catholic, Protestant, Hindu, or Jew.

The writers of Scripture tried to warn the future church of the dangers of becoming pharisee-like in nature. Time and again in Scripture love and charity are held up as being more important than anything else. In the end, neither one's background nor the temple in which one chose to worship meant much compared to the charitable acts rendered toward those less fortunate.

This theme is consistent throughout Scripture. Although all the other aspects of Christianity are important, what remains essential in the Judeo-Christian ethic is the issue of justice, which always manifests itself in how one's neighbors are treated. This is how one's Christianity is measured. James continues the same line of thinking. In his letter to the early Christian church he cautions members against believing that membership or "faith" without real social justice is acceptable:

> "What use is it if someone says he has faith and yet has nothing to show for it? Can he be saved by faith? What if a brother or sister has rags for clothes and is hungry, and one of you says, 'Peace be with you, keep yourself warm and eat heartily,' but does nothing to provide for their needs, what good is it? So it is with faith; if it does not move one to action, it is lifeless. Show me your faith without works, and I will show you my faith by proof of my works." (James 2:14–18)

When one looks at the deep hatred that separated the Jews and the Samaritans throughout their history and then looks at the chronicles of justice in both the Old Testament and the New Testament, one can see how the Samaritan motifs were clearly meant to deal with the injustice of prejudice and bigotry in the family of God.

Part II

Open Your Bibles!

I do many parish missions around the country and when I begin them, I often jokingly ask all the people present to "now open your Bibles." Of course most people just grin sort of sheepishly because there are seldom more than three of four (out the hundreds who usually attend) who have actually brought Bibles with them. The reality is that many people in the Catholic Church sadly do not spend a great deal of time reading the Bible on their own. This is in part because home Bible study has not been a great part of our Catholic tradition. Many older members of the church community can actually remember when they were told it was forbidden to read the Bible on their own because, they were told, they would not be capable of correctly understanding its contents. Although certainly more do read Scripture today than in the past, independent Bible reading is still not widely practiced in many Catholic households. In fact, some people confessed they actually felt a little intimidated by the prospect of reading the Scripture completely on their own.

God, Primitive Man, and the Bible.

Besides being afraid of Scripture, many modern day Christians are turned off by the "image" of the Old Testament—feeling that with its many antiquated laws and prohibitions, it holds little relevance to their modern world. They believe the New Testament somehow makes the Old Testament null and void. (After all, on the surface one might rather talk to the God of love and forgiveness of the New Testament, rather than converse with the God who drowned the whole world in an apparent fit of rage in the Old Testament.) The result of this avoidance often leads to a lack of understanding as to the true nature and impact Scripture can have on the modern believer.

I believe that reading the Bible is essential to deepening one's spiritual growth. Not reading Scripture is like not reading an owner's manual when it comes to spiritual upkeep. However I will admit that reading the Bible can be a little tricky and certainly open to all kinds of misinterpretations unless one keeps in mind some simple but useful tools. Before encouraging you to read the Bible, allow me to share some personal insights that might make the prospect a little less frightening.

Before going into any great detail about the Bible, I want to say a word specifically about the Old Testament. The Old Testament is a wonderful book. Its stories are colorful and its characters are rich in wisdom as well as often being flawed and at times, even a bit clueless. In other words, they are portrayed as being very human. You get to meet people who are saints and sinners, successes and failures. The Old Testament, as you have seen from the first part of the book, is also filled with stories that are at times gritty and robust. Rather than try and hide people's faults, the Old Testament often lets us see that God uses them despite their limitations, just as he uses us today. One very important factor to remember when reading the Old Testament is the times in which they were written. These were primitive and often brutal times, and much of what you read must be filtered through the lives and times in which people lived.

In the same way, the images of God were also affected by the world in which people lived. It's important to remember what life was like during the original telling of these stories. This was a time when wars were savage and there were no stipulations (ala Geneva Convention) as to how the victor treated the vanquished. The victor in many conflicts would often kill everyone including women and children, or would force whole nations into slavery. When stories of war were told, God was at the helm of battle and—as we shall discover—he appears to act in much the same way as did the people of that day. So there are examples in the Old Testament where God, like many of the warrior kings who conquered the lands, would order the death of thousands without mercy (including men, women, and children). In fact, if one took the story of Noah and the flood literally, when God seems at war against his own creation, he becomes personally responsible for the deaths of conceivably millions when he orders the great flood to kill every living thing on the earth.

For the Christian, something seems out of character when we read these stories. For most of us, our introduction to God comes through his Son, Jesus Christ. And the God about which Jesus speaks does not fit the profile of the avenging, wrathful God who kills millions, or would curse whole generations to misery and suffering for the faults of one or two individuals. But clearly that persona does reflect the times in which the earlier Scripture writers lived.

Another point to remember when reading the Old Testament is that as old as many of the stories are in the Old Testament, some of them originally date back even earlier. Most Old Testament scholars believe that many of the earliest stories from the Bible can be traced back to more primitive cultures. When we explore the story of the great flood for example, we see how one ancient myth ends up being adopted into the Bible.

I believe that all through the Old Testament we see examples of the people trying to grapple with the divine in the midst of a volatile world filled with harsh realities. It was a time when animals were killed and their blood smeared on stone altars to appease their gods or where men were killed unmercifully in battle and their wives turned into slaves and concubines. Additionally, life-spans were short (despite the symbolic Old Testament numbers with lives of supposedly five- and six-hundred years) and death could come at any time. The image of God often reflected the life and times of its writers.

What is also amazing about the all of this is that in the midst of this harsh way of life, there are also examples of tenderness, love, and justice. Contrary to everything the times would seem to dictate, there are stories told and laws written about mercy, forgiveness, and caring for strangers. Even with all of the talk of blood, revenge, and curses, which one would expect during that time in history, there also emerge stories about a powerfully loving and tremendously merciful God. This almost seems out of context with the rest of the ancient world during the time of the writing of the Old Testament. Brutality in battle by a king would not have been very surprising, but a king ordering subjects to feed the poor and the strangers would seem to be more surprising.

So I believe that there is a constant struggle going on between the concept of a God that was easy to understand in contrast with a concept that might have been more difficult to grasp. God telling his people to either kill or be killed would have been easy to accept as much of their lives were lived that way. I believe it would have been hard to comprehend treating your enemies as friends, or treating others from different tribes as you would treat someone from your own tribe. Even in the New Testament, written hundreds of years later, the concept of the merciful, forgiving God (as presented by Jesus) was difficult for many to grasp. I believe there were times when God clearly won the battle over what kind of deity he was. I believe there were other times when he lost. In those times people had him thinking and acting more like *their* kings and gods.

The Bible: Two Considerations

There are two points I found about the Bible that must be considered when one starts on the exciting journey of exploring the Scriptures. The first is that the Bible was written and translated by people and not by God. Now that is not to say the Bible isn't the word of God, it is merely to point out that it is the word of God that has been handed down and at times filtered through men trying to understand the Divine. The second is that the Scriptures were never meant to be a book of science or technology but rather a book of faith and religion. Whenever people try to take the Bible as a book written directly by God or as the source of all scientific or technological information, they invariably come to a point of conflict in which either faith or reason will to suffer.

From the outset these two points are important to remember. The Bible was written and translated by human beings during a time when science and technology were in their earliest stages; and whenever human beings are in charge of anything, there is always room for human error and personal interpretation. Therefore one must distinguish between taking the entire Bible seriously and taking it all literally. Virtually every responsible theologian I have ever read or spoken with has made these points very clear.

Failing to take into account people's cultures and lack of technological knowledge is simply unrealistic when studying a work written thousands of years ago. If the Bible is going to become a source of study and inspiration for us in the twenty-first century, it is important to be mindful of the people responsible for actually recording and translating what has come to be known today as our Bible. Additionally, one must consider the amount of time that transpired between one book of the Bible and another. Keep in mind that in the beginning, many biblical stories were simply handed down orally from generation to generation. (Important Note: By most scholarly accounts the works of the Old Testament were composed and re-edited over a thousand year period—up to about the end of the third century B.C. And it wasn't until the fourth century A.D., almost four hundred years after the death and resurrection of Christ, that the New Testament [as we know it now] was finally accepted and formally sanctioned by the Synod of Carthage in 197 A.D.)

Yet even with all the time that passed and the many translations and cultures through which the Bible passed, the Bible remains absolutely consistent when it comes to the topic of God's love and justice. From the very beginning through to the end, this theme works its way throughout the entire Bible, and comes to its fullest fruition in the Gospel message of Jesus Christ. That is why I believe you have, in both the Old Testament and the New Testament, that powerful admonishment—that when it comes to understanding the relationship between God and humankind, both Testaments proclaim that as a matter of law, loving God first, and loving your neighbor as yourself are the most important laws to remember and that on these two commandments everything else rests.

I understand that the whole question concerning just what the Bible is can be a rather sensitive one, especially to those with a more fundamentalist background. However, without a clear understanding of the importance of justice and love throughout the entire history of Scripture, the Bible can be terribly misused to justify just about anything—from racial hatred to fodder for doomsday soothsayers.

While maintaining a belief that the Bible is the inspired word of God, it is still also a book written about God, as experienced by people—not a book handwritten and delivered by God himself. I believe this understanding is crucial, particularly when studying the Old Testament.

One final note, although I don't believe it is possible (at least for me) to be totally objective when writing on topics as emotionally charged as justice and the Bible, I have tried to stick to the scriptural facts as much as possible. However, here I openly admit to more than a little personal subjectivity.

A Change in the Temperament
of the Almighty:
What Happened to God
from One Testament to the Other?

Now we need to examine the apparent change in the personality of God from one Testament to the other. God went from what one theologian called a "warrior god," to a God of infinite forgiveness and mercy. Now strong elements of that forgiving nature were always present in the Old Testament as well, but clearly there was also another side to this God. Everyone who knew him knew not to provoke him. Those that didn't know him found out the hard way that one bad deed could get you and generations of your lineage into a whole world of hurt and suffering. There are stories and songs in the Old Testament that tell of the tremendous love people felt for God, as they obviously felt that love coming *from* him as well.

> "For paying attention to these laws and being careful in observing them, the LORD your God will keep his covenant of mercy as he promised to your forebears." (Deuteronomy 7:12)

> "But you are a God that forgives; full of grace and with compassion, slow to anger, and abundant in mercy and love." (Nehemiah 9:17)

> "I am as an olive tree in God's house, trusting in God's unending love." (Psalm 52:10)

> "You, O Lord, are a God of mercy and grace; you are not swift to anger, but faithful and loving." (Psalm 86:15).

Psalm 136 is an entire love song about God and his unfailing and everlasting love. Here are just five of the twenty-six verses written about this loving God.

"Offer thanks to the LORD, who is good; God's love is enduring and unending; offer thanks to the God of gods. His love
endures forever; offer thanks to the Lord of lords; forever his
love endures. It is God alone who has done deeds of great
wonder, forever his love endures. It is God who made the
heavens, forever his love endures . . ." (Psalm 136:1–5)

But the Scriptures go on to show quite vividly that while he may have been "not swift to anger" and "faithful and loving," once you got him riled, he could be a challenge to be around. How does this God go from being hailed as one whose love endures forever, to a God who would curse a king and all of his people for daring to show mercy by sparing the life of another king whose whole army he had just defeated?

"Because you freed the man I sentenced to death, your life will
be taken in exchange for his life, your people for his people."
(1 Kings 20:42)

Consider the dismissing of Saul as king of Israel because he failed to slaughter all of King Amalek's people, including his woman and children, as God had demanded.

"Go forth and attack the Amalekites and annihilate everything
they own. Don't spare them; kill men, women, children,
infants, cattle, sheep, camels, and donkeys." (1 Samuel 15:3)

"Because you have rejected the directives of the LORD, he has
rejected you as king." (1 Samuel 15:23)

But those are only tiny fits of temper compared to one of the most well-known stories in the Bible. How does a God of mercy kill an entire world in a flood?

To people more familiar with the New Testament, this clearly doesn't sound like the loving and merciful God of Jesus Christ. What happened? Theologians and scripture scholars have been talking about this for years.

Some attribute this apparent shift in God's personality not so much to God himself, but as said earlier, to the ancient peoples who filtered their stories of God *through* their own sense of right and wrong. Others believe that God did go through a change of heart, vowing to give up his warrior-like ways in favor of a more merciful approach. There are some who even believe that one of the reasons God came into the world as a man (i.e., Jesus Christ) was to atone not only for our sins, but to atone for his own past behavior by submitting himself, totally defenseless to the cross. Some of that stuff can get pretty heavy. My goal here is to get you to read the Bible, not to make you even more intimidated. From all that I have read and my own personal feelings, I think this apparent personality change might be attributed to three things:

- One was the point already made—the lack of understanding by ancient peoples about the physical nature of the world in which they lived, thus witnessing events like lightening or earthquakes and assuming that God had a harsh and dangerous side.

- The second was also touched upon—the shaping of God into a human deity, i.e., someone who would relate to the world much like most humans did during that period in history. (There used to be an old saying that "God made man in his own image, and man returned the favor.")

- But the third might be found in what the Chinese called the *Yin* and the *Yang*. In other words, the human need for balance.

Yin and Yang

Chinese philosophers in the fourth century B.C. began writing about the *Yin* and the *Yang* as opposing forces in nature that kept all things in balance. The *Yin* was associated with the darker side of nature, while the *Yang* was associated with the lighter side.

"By the end of that century *yin* became associated with everything dark, moist, receptive, earthy, and female, whereas *yang* was bright, dry, active, heavenly, and male. *Yin* and *yang* were believed to combine in various proportions to produce all the different objects in the universe." (*Microsoft® Encarta® Reference Library 2003* © 1993–2002, Microsoft Corporation. All rights reserved.)

The ancient Chinese were not the only ones to come up with this perspective. Greek philosophers came up with their own version of *Yin* and *Yang*. It was believed that all things needed to be in balance in order to work properly. Even poets often wrote about the importance of balance.

> "Without contraries there is no progression. Attraction and repulsion, reason and energy, love and hate, are necessary to human existence." —William Blake (1757–1827) British poet, painter, engraver, and mystic

I believe the struggle people have always had with God is that the more he becomes known, the more that balance seems lacking, at least in the way human beings understand the natural order of things. In the New Testament, stories of God's love rarely have attached to them that familiar warning of consequence if not heeded, as was often the case in the Old Testament. In the New Testament, God reaches out to his people with love with his right hand, but doesn't appears to have the balancing hammer or sword of punishment in his left hand. If God's ultimate goodness is the *Yang*, then by the natural order of the universe many believed, the *Yin* of God must be filled with ruthless retribution. It would seem only natural. If God would go through all of the trouble of bringing his people out of the darkness of slavery, then surely one could at least be expected to precisely follow his rules. If not, why wouldn't this powerful God deal with you the same way he dealt with your enemies? That would only seem fair. Some may have thought that if one disobeys God, would not that make you an enemy of God as well?

In the New Testament we become conditioned to hearing about "unconditional love." But in the Old Testament it seemed as though God's love was very conditional. Let's return to the previously cited quote from Deuteronomy:

> "**For** paying attention to these laws **and being careful** in observing them, the LORD your God **will** keep his covenant of mercy as he promised to your forebears." (Deuteronomy 7:12)

Here God's love seems to be given based on one's obedience. It seems clearly conditional. If you do as you are told, you will be loved. But if that's the case, what happens if you do not do as you are told? The answer is quite simple. Just read down another line or two in that passage mentioned and the answer is plain. By saying what he won't do if you do obey, he clearly tells you what he will do if you do not:

> "The LORD will protect you and keep you free from all illness. He will not plague you with any of the awful afflictions that you knew in Egypt. Instead he will inflict them on all who oppose you." (Deuteronomy 7:15)

One can detect the thinly veiled threat contained in this passage. God is clearly saying that if you do as I say, I won't do to you what I did to them.

Some in the past argued that God still loved you, even when he was thrashing you to within an inch of your life, and putting a curse on you and all of your people for generation upon generation. But one can understand how many modern-day believers might find that kind of thinking hard to accept in the twenty-first century, particularly in light of the kind of love shown by this same God in the New Testament.

To add to the confusion about this whole question of balance, we cannot forget that life was continuing to happen around ancient men and woman and that life could include wars, fires, droughts, and any number of other natural and unnatural disasters. Most likely, ancient people would not have had a clue as to the origin or cause of these events. Even the people who did their best to serve God might still be affected by life's ups and downs including diseases, famines, and floods.

So how might primitive cultures try and bring into balance a God whose "love is enduring and without end" with a world that is often cruel and war-like? Consider when people would see a bolt of lightening strike a tree and start a fire that burns down a whole village. Or how might they try and explain children born crippled or blind? Or finding themselves suddenly overrun by foreign tribes and seeing their people carried away into slavery? To primitive societies the answer was fairly simple. If it was God who brought them good, then it must be God who brought them misery. If it was God who brought them rain, it must be God who brought them drought. If it was God who blessed them in the good times, it must be God who was cursing them in the bad times. Most humans, even the ancients learned early that almost everything had two sides to it. Fire is good, but it can burn you. Water is necessary for life, but you can also drown in it. Food is important, but if spoiled it can make you sick (and in ancient times it could easily kill you). A philosopher once said that nothing can be sliced so thin that there is only one side to it. God is a god of limitless life and mercy, but surely for the sake of balance, there must be another side. And that side must be as dark as his goodness is light. That is, after all, what balance is all about, the *Yin* and the *Yang*.

Knowing how powerful this God was in his love, one would do everything possible to avoid feeling the power of his vengeance. Perhaps that is why, after experiencing the power of God's love during the exodus, the people put together such stringent laws, trying to stay on his good side. By the time they were through, you could be stoned, beaten, or sold into slavery for such a minor offense as mixing fibers when making a garment. Since it was believed that God was not above punishing just an individual but the entire community for one individual's crime, people became rather quick triggered when it came to meeting out punishment. It was as if they wanted God to see that they were as upset as they believed he was. Some might argue that rather than believing that God was doing the punishing, it was Satan and evil spirits that were to blame. But the devil is not mentioned quite as prominently in the Old Testament as in the New Testament. It seems quite clear that if God was after you, he took care of you himself. He didn't leave that to anyone else.

Love in the New Testament: Upsetting the Balance.

In the New Testament God (through Jesus) completely upsets the balance. God's love is not only unconditional but at time it appears to be one sided. In Paul's beautiful definition of love (as he understands it from Jesus), love has none of the "downside" that is common in so many things. In defining God's love, Paul seeks to remove all the negative elements that one could have applied to the God of the Old Testament. Anger, jealousy, holding grudges are all gone from Paul's definition of love:

> "Love is patient, love is kind. It is not envious and it does not boast. Love is not rude nor is it self-seeking. Love is not quick to anger nor does it keep a journal of wrongdoings. Love does not find joy in evil; rather it delights in the truth. Love protects, believes, hopes, and perseveres in all things." (1 Corinthians 13:4–7)

It's important to understand that there is a drastic change in the perception of God and primarily in one direction. As stated earlier, countless generations sang of the beauty and power of God's love. In the New Testament they continue to sing of his great love. However, what's missing is the anger, the fierceness, and the vindictiveness. It not like God turned three hundred and sixty degrees, only one hundred and eighty! Now God is not merely a god who loves, he becomes Love itself:

> "We know and trust in the love God has for us. God is love and whoever is steadfast in love lives in God and God in him." (1 John 4:16)

And fear is no longer to be a part of the equation:

> "Love is not fearful. Love that is perfect drives out fear as fear is related to punishment . . ." (1 John 4:18)

I wanted to explore this issue of putting the balanced face on God before going back to the Old Testament and particularly the story about the great flood (which I wish to talk about in detail). There is real danger in not understanding how this image may have come about and some of these reasons God may have gotten this reputation in the first place. If people believe that, in the cause of righteousness, God can be brutal and even unmerciful— that kind of thinking can give people the excuse they need to act in similar ways in the cause of their own definitions of "righteousness." It can produce disastrous results. I believe we see this happening today in many places around the world. People claiming to be acting in the name of God, are causing havoc among the human family. It's harder to destroy people in the name of God, when the Gospel is telling everyone to love one another regardless of where they are from or the language they speak. It's easier when people believe God is saying that he kills when he is angry and therefore others are commanded to do likewise in his cause and in his name.

Revelation: A Return to God's Old Form?

I remember watching television one evening when a popular preacher delivered a sermon on the Book of Revelation. Since the Book of Revelation is the last book in the Bible, it was both amazing and chilling to hear the conclusions this Christian minister drew from that single book. Consider again for a moment the words of Jesus:

> "You have heard, 'An eye for an eye and a tooth for a tooth.' But I tell you, do not resist an evildoer. If you are struck on your right cheek, offer him your left one as well. If someone wants to sue you for your garment, give him your coat as well. If someone should urge you to go one mile, go two miles. You have heard the adage 'Love your neighbor and hate your enemy.' But I tell you, love your enemies and pray for all those who might persecute you. May you be children of your heavenly Father, as this is the Father that causes the sun to rise on the evil and the good and sends rain to fall on the righteous and the unrighteous. If you love those who love you, what reward will you have? Even tax collectors do the same." (Matthew 5:38–47)

One could tell from the fiery sermons this televangelist was known for, that the idea of "turning the other cheek" clearly must have felt unsatisfying and flat out wrong. All of Jesus' life represented a new way of thinking. As stated earlier, Paul (in Romans) told us it would not be satisfying or even doable without the power of the Holy Spirit to lift us above our human nature. This preacher found what he believed to be a loophole to all of this "other cheek business" in the Book of Revelation. It gave him a chance to feel that God was returning to the good old days where enemies were slain and the unrighteous received their just desserts. On television he said that he hoped when he died and went to be with Jesus, that Jesus would grant him a wish.

He believed that at the end of time, Jesus was coming back and he would be heading an army of angels. He said that when this happened, blood would run in the streets. (I am paraphrasing, but he actually said this.) And his one wish was that Jesus would give him a sword and allow him to help smite the non-believers. He wanted to help kill those who did not believe in the God of love and mercy.

Where did he get this idea? I imagine it could be from the ninth chapter of the Book of Revelation when it states:

> "Then the sixth angel sounded his trumpet and I heard a voice coming from the horns of the golden altar that was before God. It told the sixth angel who had the trumpet, 'Release the four angels who are bound at the river Euphrates.' The four angels who had been kept ready were released to kill a third of all humankind. The number of troops was two hundred million . . ." (Revelation 9:13–16)

It is hard for me to imagine someone who is a believer in Jesus taking this literally and wanting to be in the forefront of the carnage. If God was going to send an army of angels to wipe out a third of the earth, that would mean that he was going to literally slaughter at least 2.1 billion people, considering the world's population today (roughly 6.5 billion). Who knows what the world's population might be by the time of the *perusia* (from Greek meaning "to be caught up, taken away, whisked away out of sight," also termed 'The Rapture').

Here again one can see the dangers of not knowing the simple truth of God's love as spelled out in the New Testament. There is the reality that the love is unconditional and despite all that we might deserve, his grace is without additional price and is in fact amazing. Through Jesus, God makes plain his ambitions, to love the world, and to teach it through that love (not through force and violence), that love is the only way to truly live and grow. But that is still not easy for humans to accept, even though the news should be wonderful and blessed. That's why the Book of Revelation, despite all that Jesus taught the world through his life, his teachings, and his death, still holds hope for some that God will work things out the old fashion way—with good, old-fashioned punishment. Only then might some feel that there is some balance in Christ's message. Some might say, "Jesus is merciful and full of forgiveness, but if you don't accept that mercy, you can and should receive the other side of mercy (punishment)." But just like the stories in the Old Testament, such as those of Noah and Jonah, you can only get something out of a book like Revelation if you can look past the literal and see it through the prism of the Gospels.

A Closer Look

What is the Book of Revelation all about? It is a book that has had scholars debating that question for years. We know that it was written at a time when the early church was under extreme duress due to the oppressive treatment by the Roman Empire toward early Christians. After the Emperor Nero (as it was rumored) burned the city of Rome and blamed it on the Christians, the early church was severely oppressed. After Nero's death, the new emperor Domitian (81–96 A.D.) seemed determined to be as ruthless towards the early Christians as was his predecessor. It is believed that much of the Book of Revelation was written in a code, using known imagery out of the Old Testament to communicate to the early church two important facts:

- One was that they should not give up hope and should stay true to the message of Jesus.
- Second, just as God had always done in the past he will be victorious over the evil that was confronting them during their time in history. And even though he might not use the same methods as he employed in the past, the results will be the same.

John wanted the early church to remember that God had the power, the strength, and the might to completely obliterate the forces of oppression that seemed omnipotent to the early Christians. It didn't matter how powerful the emperor's army was, because God had the power to kill an entire third of the world with a single blast of a horn if it was his desire to do so. Even the emperor and all his legions still pale under the power of God—and compared to God's power, the emperor was no match at all.

John also wanted the new church to remember all of the pain and suffering that early Christians had endured because Rome hoped it would cause them to give up their belief in Christ. It was an exercise in futility. As always, God would prevail.

But one can only imagine how much more suffering the early church would have had to endure if such a message were circulated around the Roman Empire using straightforward language. Thus John used coded symbols and language that he believed the early church would have understood.

When read in that light, the beauty of the Book of Revelation becomes apparent. The message of remaining faithful to Jesus (despite hardship) is not a message of dire warnings and carnage but one of comfort and strength. But taking the Book of Revelation as a literal prediction of how God is going to destroy the world is an exercise counterproductive to the Gospel message. In the introduction to the Book of Revelation in the New American Bible it states:

"The book of Revelation had its origin in a time of crisis, but it remains valid and meaningful for Christians of all time. In the face of apparently insuperable evil, either from within or from without, all Christians are called to trust in Jesus' promise, 'Behold I am with you always, until the end of the age' (Matthew 28:20). Those who remain steadfast in their faith and confidence in the risen Lord need have no fear. Suffering, persecution, even death by martyrdom, though remaining impenetrable mysteries of evil, do not comprise an absurd dead end. No matter what adversity or sacrifice Christians may endure, they will in the end triumph over Satan and his forces because of their fidelity to Christ the victor. This is the enduring message of the book; it is a message of hope and consolation and challenge for all who dare to believe."

"This book contains an account of visions in symbolic and allegorical language borrowed extensively from the Old Testament, especially Ezekiel, Zechariah, and Daniel . . . This much, however, is certain: symbolic descriptions are not to be taken as literal descriptions, nor is the symbolism meant to be pictured realistically. One would find it difficult and repulsive to visualize a lamb with seven horns and seven eyes: yet Jesus Christ is described in precisely such words (Revelation 5 and 6). The author used these images to suggest Christ's universal (seven) power (horns) and knowledge (eyes).—*New American Bible*, Catholic Study Edition.

The language is "symbolic and allegorical," and is meant to be understood both by the early suffering Christians (who would have made the connection of metaphors such as the "beast" and the oppressive Roman regime), and Christians today who need to remember that in our darkest days, God is still in control.

Once again in this modern day of science we can appreciate the poetic language without having to grapple with things such as:

"In the sky the star fell to the earth as figs not yet ready for harvest being jarred loose from a fig tree enduring a mighty wind." (Revelation 6:13)

Likewise, there is the knowledge that if the stars ever did fall from the sky, they would crush the earth like a twig.

We are also allowed to see (through all the necessary harsh and strident language) the constant love and comfort that comes from a compassionate God:

> "For this reason they who are before the throne of God offer praise to him day and night in his holy place. He who sits on the throne will provide cover for them. They will never hunger or thirst again. The sun will not beat down upon them, for the Lamb at the center of the throne will be their shepherd; he will lead them to springs of living water. God will faithfully remove the tears from their eyes." (Revelation 7:15–17)

It is important to look at a book such as Revelation not only through the eyes of the original recipients but also through the eyes of twenty-first century Christians. Today there are reasons why we would never consider stoning someone to death who disagrees with our faith, nor would we consider scarifying live animals and spreading their blood over our houses as protection from death or pestilence. And yet some of the lessons we might draw from ancient biblical texts such as Revelation are as necessary and as relevant today as they would have been when they were written. Without the safeguards of the over-riding message of the Gospels, other messages that might be drawn from the text could produce disastrous results—results that in today's world of instant communications and deadly weaponry could spell disaster of a horrifying magnitude. That's why it is important to distinguish between language and message. The language used to communicate with a people in the early stages of development can vary greatly from the language used to talk to modern people. The message given in the New Testament clearly and unequivocally tells us today (as well as the early church) that love and not violence is the commandment given to us by God through Christ. Nothing in Revelation or any other book in the Bible should be seen as refuting that message.

In certain airline magazines there is a popular business guru who claims that you don't get what you deserve—you get what you negotiate. Through Christ, we sinners no longer get what we deserve; we get what was negotiated on the cross on our behalf through unlimited love and forgiveness. That might not feel right to many Christians, but it certainly should feel good.

Why Is This Important?
Ancient Understandings
of the Physical World—
Different yet the Same

It is obvious that we are vastly different from our ancestors. We are a people with a huge scientific and technological arsenal of information at our disposal. We have the knowledge to approach matters of science and space in a more objective manner. Ancient societies depended more on beliefs passed down from generation to generation (without the scientific ability to check and crosscheck information). We must not forget that in many ancient societies, questioning established beliefs was rewarded with a death sentence.

We now have the ability to measure the amount of time it takes for planets to evolve and moons to be created. We now know many of the causes of mental and physical disorders that can render a person lame, blind, or emotionally disturbed. Unlike ancient societies who believed that all occurrences, whether good or bad, were the direct result of some divine reward or punishment, we have a better understanding of the earth, the universe, and how it all works together. We now have the means to explore worlds that were totally invisible to biblical men and women (e.g., the world of cells and atoms). This knowledge gives us an opportunity to see some aspects of the biblical writers' world in a light that is clearer to us than perhaps it even was to them. This awareness of how physical things around us work can tremendously help our faith and understanding in a God whom we have come to know and love rather than fear.

We do not have to keep God in the limited circle of knowledge that was a reality for ancient men and women. We can ask questions and explore the relationships between God, faith, love, and the universe. I believe this is very important in understanding a God of justice and love, and in seeing how the earlier stories portraying God fit into the scientific world of the twenty-first century.

The point I wish to make here is that understanding the world of the scriptural authors in this light can provide a valuable learning tool for believers. First, it can let us concentrate on the moral and theological issues of God's word without getting hung-up on technicalities. By this I mean such things as exact dates or events that could have been the result of natural phenomena, things that the Bible was never really meant to address—or was capable of so doing. Second, it serves as a historical perspective on how far we have come technologically as a people, while at the same time showing us how much we haven't grown morally or socially as a society, thus making the topics the Bible addresses as timely as ever.

Technological Growth versus Human Growth

There are few technicians of the year 47 AD who would find their skills of any great use in the twenty-first century. However, almost every Greek philosopher could teach Philosophy 101 in most modern universities without much trouble. B.F. Skinner states:

> "Greek physics and biology are now of historical interest only (no modern physicist or biologist would turn to Aristotle for help), but the dialogues of Plato are still assigned to students and cited as if they threw light on human behavior. Aristotle could not have understood a page of modern physics or biology, but Socrates and his friends would have little trouble in following most current discussion of human affairs." (*Beyond Freedom and Dignity* [New York: Alfred A. Knopf, 1971] pp. 5–6)

Despite what some may wish to argue, there are few scholars today who would press to uphold Genesis as an actual, literal account of creation. By a simple process of the most elementary science, one can see how the story of the world being created in six days as described in Genesis is impossible since we now know that a day happens as the result of the earth rotating around its axis every twenty four hours. We know that what separates day from night is the position of the earth towards the sun at any given time during that rotation. We also know that what makes a week is the position of the earth towards the sun as it rotates around the sun. We know what makes a year is the earth's complete rotation around the sun, which we now know takes fifty-two weeks—three hundred and sixty five days. So time itself is measured by the position of the earth as it rotates on its axis and the position of the earth as it rotates around the sun.

However, the first three days of the creation account could not have been twenty four hour days, or even days as measured by the rotation of the earth or its orbit around the sun—since according to Genesis, the sun was not created until the fourth day. Plus we also know that stars were not merely lights in the sky put there to light up the earth at night. We now know that most stars are in fact like our own sun, yet millions of light years away.

> "God made two great lights in the sky, the greater light to govern the day and the lesser light to govern the night. God also he made the stars and set them in the breadth of the sky to provide light upon the earth, to govern the day and the night and to separate the time of light from the time of darkness. God saw that it was good. And then there was evening and then there was morning—the fourth day." (Genesis 1:16–19)

In his book, Missionary of the Sacred Heart Michael Maher begins by saying:

> "Although the opening chapter of Genesis was long regarded as a factual account of the origin of the world and of the human family, it is now almost universally recognized as primarily a profession of faith, a poetic affirmation of Israel's religious convictions. Any attempt to reconcile the data of this chapter with the findings of modern science is misguided and futile." (*Genesis* [Wilmington, DE: Michael Glazier, 1992])

But does this mean that men and women living in the twenty-first century must dismiss God's role in creating the universe? I don't believe so. Millions of informed and educated Christians recite a Christian profession of faith during their worship services. In one form or another, it begins by acknowledging a belief that God created the heavens and the earth. People believe this primarily as a matter of faith, not as a matter of science. People use the Bible as an instrument of knowledge concerning the everlasting power and love of the God in whom they believe. No one would go to the Bible to prove the existence of black holes in the universe or to establish weather, or the veracity of $E=mc^2$. The Bible would be an outdated book if we relied on it to help us solve modern scientific mathematical equations.

Since the Bible is primarily meant to deal with the questions of faith, morality, and social behavior—or, perhaps a better way of stating it, the questions of Socrates and not the problems of Aristotle—it is still as timeless as ever, considering how little we've changed in those areas. We still have poverty and wars and many of our brothers and sisters still feel the weight of oppression on their shoulders.

Let's Take a Look at that Flood

Our understanding of how the ancient writers perceived God is as important to this work as it allows us a better perspective of this God to whom John gave the name *Love* and to whom justice was so important. It helps us dispel what the early biblical writers perceived as an evil and dangerously impetuous side of God. And mentioned in a previous chapter, upon study it becomes clear that the perception of this fierce, angry, and jealous side may have became a way of explaining why things like floods, disease, and natural disasters occurred. As well, it was an attempt to add some balance to this God who may have seemed too good to be true. How would ancient man explain an epidemic such as smallpox wiping out whole villages—except to say that God was angry and punishing everyone. Humans have always needed some kind of answer to the questions of life, death, and the inexplicable. Whenever getting answers wasn't available, God (or the gods) was either given credit or blame. Ancient men and women needed to know "why," just as modern men and women seek to know "why." But again there is an inherent danger in believing that the God you worship is capable of displaying his anger in hostile ways—in the name of holiness. For me, the story of the great flood exemplifies that if pushed, God seemed capable of doing an exorbitant amount of deadly violence.

How might a story like the flood make it into the Bible in the first place? One possible explanation is oral traditions. Many great stories and legends were often passed orally from generation to generation. It is also important to understand that many of these stories (such as the flood) can be found in other religions. The story of the great flood is believed to have its beginning in the ancient Mesopotamian account of creation. In the story of Atrahasis, humans are created as laborers to do the work which upper-class gods were demanding from lower-class gods, thus sparking a rebellion in the heavens. In what is undoubtedly the first recorded instance of noise pollution as well as over-population, the humans offended the gods by their explosive spread and resulting noise. The introduction to the Book of Genesis in the *New Jerome Biblical Commentary* states:

> "By a succession of plagues culminating in a great flood that wipes out everyone except Utnapishtim, a divine favorite, the

gods finally put an end to the disturbance. From the surviving man a fresh beginning is made, this time with inbuilt safeguards against the untrammeled population growth that led to disaster. The similarity of the Atrahasis plot to Genesis 2—9 is clear; equally clear is the biblical nuance in the details . . . The biblical writers have produced a version of a common Mesopotamian story of the origins of the populated world, exploring major questions about God and humanity through narrative." (*Reissue edition* [New York: Prentice Hall, 1989])

It seems obvious that stories such as the great flood were handed down not only in Judaism, but many other religions also shared some of these stories.

Today we can understand better how ancient cultures borrowed from one another's legends and fables as they attempted to understand the grand schemes of the divine. Perhaps the story of an actual flood destroying an entire city might, after being passed through generations, eventually evolve to be a story where the whole world was destroyed. We must keep in mind that to ancient civilizations, the world would have seemed like a much smaller place than it actually was. Remember, until the time of Columbus, there was a belief that the world only went so far—like the top of a table and then it just stopped. The common fear was that if you sailed into the ocean, you would eventually just fall off the edge of the earth. Early man's idea of the size of the world and his limited knowledge of the workings of nature could have contributed much toward the evolution of stories—all before being recorded in the Book of Genesis. In today's world we can derive a moral from a story such as Noah and the flood. We can do this without having to believe that one day God became so angry that he literally destroyed the entire population of the whole world—including infants and children, elderly men and women, and people who were sick or suffering. Nor do we need to believe that he chose drowning as a means to teach the world a lesson, an especially frightening and agonizing way to die, drawn out over a span of forty days and nights.

"The earth had grown to be corrupt in God's eyes and people lacked respect for the law. God saw the earth had become corrupt as people lived lives of depravity. God said to Noah, 'I am going to end the lives of all earthly mortals as the earth is filled with violence because of them. I am going to destroy them and life on the earth . . . I am going to cause floodwaters on the earth to destroy all life and every creature that has breath. Everything on earth will perish.'" (Genesis 6:11–13, 17)

Think for a moment the literal meaning of the destruction of "every creature that has breath." Could one imagine what it would have been like to watch helplessly as water poured into shelters over days, rising up to peoples ankles then their hips and finally up to their necks—all over the course of forty days? By such an account, it would not only seem that God wanted to destroy his creation, but also wanted them to suffer hopelessly in fear and agony until the moment of death. Consider those moments in the movie *Titanic* where mothers held their trapped babies above the waterline. There were also those that held their children close to them while the waters surged up, knowing all hope was lost. We would have to imagine it would be a rather cruel deity that would put a whole world through such torturous deaths. Even though there might be some who would still endorse the practice, as a society we don't even condone torturing criminals, a practice most people consider to be inhumane. Would a loving God really bring torturous death to an entire living planet? Most people, filled with sin and imperfections, would never consider doing such a dastardly deed. How then does one rationalize a God of purest love that could commit such an act?

Another puzzling question is how the whole world could—save one family—go so wrong as to warrant death on such a massive scale? Yet the creator of that world bore no responsibility whatsoever for its behavior? Why would God want to destroy everything, including "every creature that has breath?"

If we are to accept the story as fact, the answers to these questions would be most troubling to most modern-day Christians. Because the answer would appear either to be God—with all of his outward appearances of love—has a really cruel streak running through him, or he is a firm believer in the old adage "do as I say and not as I do." Although there was a time when parents could raise their children using that kind of logic, in today's world most parents know that they must lead by example and not just through force.

But It's Still a Really Good Story

I'm not asserting that the story of Noah is not an important and powerful one with strong religious themes and morals. Symbolically, it can be a wonderful story about one family's persistent faith in God despite what the rest of the world may believe. Even if the whole world "drowns" in its own sinfulness, one family remained steadfast in its belief in God. Even while feeling completely shut off from the rest of the world, their faith in God sustained them until God brought them through it all. God will surely continue to do so, not just for Noah, but for all that believe. It can also be a powerful hymn of praise to the awesome power of God. It serves as a reminder that God is stronger than all the hate, violence, and darkness in the world. Surely one person's faith in the God of light and hope can withstand a flood of darkness and fear, even if the whole world seems to succumb to it. Understanding the story metaphorically makes it much easier to derive a moral teaching. It is an impossibly difficult task to reconcile a God who seems to hate the whole world so much that he kills it, and yet loves the world so much that he gives to it his most precious possession—his only son—in order to save it. Accepting the story as a metaphor, we no longer have to stretch our imagination to figure out:

- how Noah became a father at 500 years of age;
- how he put two of every creature in the world on a boat that was only 450 feet long;
- and included every kind of food on the earth;
- and did it all at 600 years of age in one week!

This is one example of the dilemma modern-day Christians face when reading the Old Testament. They feel that they are not being true to God's word if they wonder about a story such as Noah's, especially when they are told they must accept it literally. They may choose to stay away from the Old Testament totally—thereby robbing themselves of some of the most powerful and beautiful works in Scripture. This is why it is so important to read the Old Testament with the knowledge of the New Testament so that one can see who God really is, and how important love and forgiveness is (and has always been) to this God. We can see that he never asks people to do what he is not prepared to do himself. Perhaps that is one of the most important points of the whole incarnation. It is God making visible not only his love, but also his empathy with creation. God—through Jesus—walks the paths of fear, frustration, anger, and loneliness, and yet he still insists on loving and promoting justice. He is not *separate from* creation but is *part of* creation. He becomes, at once, both creator and creation, loving and caring for that creation through it all. As *son*, he demands of himself as *father*, mercy and forgiveness (cf. Luke 23:34), even as he hangs on a cross. At no time does he demand vengeance for the wickedness that is happening to him. It would be hard to imagine what evil a world could have done prior to the execution of Jesus that could have hurt God greater than the murder of his Son. And still he does not deliver destruction as an act of retribution, but instead forgives as an act of kindness. That is what makes this God endearing and important in the everyday lives of people.

Love versus Fear

Another factor in the matter of love versus fear is its importance as a learning tool to the growing child. In modern psychology we are told when a relationship is based on fear, most healthy people will stay in that relationship only as long as it takes for them to get the courage leave it. People who stay in that type of relationship (once they have a means of leaving it) are considered unhealthy. As people grow older, wiser, and amass more resources, they outgrow fear-based relationships. The same is true with gods. Belief in many of the ancient gods who held their followers in the iron grip of fear is now extinct because people grew weary of their ways and grew beyond their dependency on such deities. I believe a perfect example of this is the gods of ancient Greece. Most people are aware of the great mythological gods of ancient Greece such as Apollo and Zeus. While they had many great attributes, they all suffered from a common flaw—they appeared to have human weaknesses. Let's face it, human weakness coupled with the power of a god can be a lethal combination. The Greek gods were thought to be capable of jealousy, anger, and even petty behavior. The results could be disastrous for the mortals who were unfortunate enough to be in their charge. If provoked, these (potentially) wrath-filled deities could rain down terror on villages whole towns, sometimes unleashing terrible plagues or horrible monsters such as mythological sea creatures the size and the temperament of a Godzilla. These gods could love you one moment and could just as quickly turn on you the next moment. They could curse you with deformities or strike you dead. Thus was the power they wielded over their followers and it worked for centuries until people began to "grow up." Once that happened, people rejected belief in gods who could take such liberties with their lives, and do so simply because they possessed the power of gods. There were other things that led to their downfall—including for many—learning about the God of Jesus Christ. But becoming fed up with the intolerable behavior of their gods had much to do with the eventual demise of beliefs in Greek gods by the ancient people.

One could ask why the Israelites never abandoned their God, considering he could act at times with apparent cruelty to his people. Most scholars believe it was because of the covenant agreement mentioned earlier in this book. The people of Israel were not a people who simply worshiped a god, they believed they were in fact one with their God and therefore inseparable from him. They believed that his identity and theirs was so intricately tied together that as a people, they would cease to exist if they were separated from his presence. As the temple was the living symbol of his presence among them, they could not imagine life without this God, no matter what he did to them. When the people of this God found themselves in pain and destruction, feeling betrayed by their God, (e.g., when Jerusalem was destroyed and the people were marched into slavery), they still could not bring themselves to turn against him. It seemed this God had not only abandoned them, but actively took part in their destruction. So the only option open to them was to believe that somehow God, like a stern father who sometimes must punish his children, still loved them and was still in control of the world. It was, perhaps with a heavy heart, what he thought needed to be done to them for their own good. It was unthinkable to think that he had somehow abandoned them or had lost control of the world. The author Jack Miles writes:

> "According to the received theocracy, first formulated after Israel was conquered by Assyria and Babylonia, that double defeat did not mean what it seemed to mean. The Lord's victory over Egypt had been a real victory, but his apparent defeat by Assyria and Babylonia was not a real defeat. No, Assyria and Babylonia were actually tools in the hands of the Lord who, far from defeated, was in perfect control of events and merely punishing Israel for its sins. Painful as it might seem to accept the claim that a national god who had once been so favorable had now turned hostile, the alternative was the loss of that god as a potential future support and protection. Since Israel's sense of itself as a people had become inseparable from its sense of covenant with the Lord, life with him even in an angry and punitive mood was preferable to life altogether without him."

(*Christ: A Crisis in the Life of God* [New York: Vintage, 2002]
Part II: "A Prophet Against the Promise")

But even in Israel some of the people had their fill of a god who could
act so ruthlessly at will. Miles continues:

> "True, it may be more painful to imagine that there is no god
> or that, if there is, you are beneath his notice than to imagine
> that your god is ruthlessly punitive. After all, a god who pun-
> ishes may later reward. A god who is in control of the world
> order, whatever it is, may someday improve it. If this is com-
> fort, however, it is cold comfort; and there were clearly some
> in ancient Israel who were not willing to wait for it indefi-
> nitely." (Op. cit.)

Being a stern and vengeful "father god" eventually will not play well
with any child who grows up, even if that child is creation itself. In today's
world we learn that parents who feed and clothe their children and share
with them great moments of tenderness and love, still do not have the right
to beat their children when they get angry, just because they are their parents. So there has to be more to God's actions than early civilization could
hope to understand. Clearly God knew this, as all young things grow up,
even humanity.

Ham, Son of Noah
It is so important to realize how the themes of love and justice never
wavered in Scripture—no matter what period of time the Bible was going
through. Without this understanding, people can take some of the more
primitive notions of God and the world, and turn them into modern day
disasters. One of the best (or perhaps worst) examples is the ninth chapter
of Genesis. It tells how scriptural testimony of love and justice can be
ignored in favor of a symbolic and misunderstood biblical story.
Interestingly enough, it again has to do with the story of our friend Noah
after the flood. The story tells how Noah, after working in the field one day,
drank some wine, got drunk, and fell asleep naked in his tent. One of his
sons, Ham, the father of Canaan, walked into the tent, saw his father, turned
and walked outside to tell his two brothers what he had seen. His two brothers,
Shem and Japheth, then entered the tent, walking backwards, presumably so as

not to see their father's nakedness, and they covered him with a blanket. The account continues:

> "When Noah awakened from his drunken sleep, he learned what his youngest son had done. He said, 'Cursed be Canaan, he shall be the lowest slave to his brothers.' . . . 'Bless, O LORD, Shem's tents, may Canaan be his slave, and may God extend Japheth bounds so that he, too, will dwell in the tents of Shem. Let Canaan be his slave, as well'" (Genesis 9:24–27)

The story goes on, recounting that Ham had four sons, Egypt, Canaan, Cush, and Put, who went on the become the legendary founders of the countries or people that bore their names. The Cushites were a black tribe that settled in southern Egypt, and many believe they were the ancestors of the Ethiopians. The legend also suggests that Put went on to father Libya.

Anyone who studies the writings of this period understands the symbolism and style used by the authors. Many biblical scholars, including the editors of the *New English Bible, Oxford Study Edition*, suggest that one of the things the writers were doing was giving themselves a theological justification for the conquest of Canaan and the taking of many of the Canaanites into slavery. Again, Michael Maher makes some interesting points on the subject:

> "In this curious account Ham must be seen as the representative of the Canaanites who preceded the Israelites as the occupants of Palestine . . . The actual curse which envisages Canaan as a slave to his brothers was probably formulated at a time when the Canaanites were actually subject to their "brothers," the Israelites who were descended from Shem." (Maher, Op. cit.)

Others suggest that part of the story is meant to give names to the three great divisions of people who were known to the ancient writers of Genesis. This was a common practice of the period in which Genesis was written. An example is the story about Rome being founded by two brothers, Romulus and Remus.

However, since according to legend, all the "sons of Ham" settled in or near Africa, for years people believed that all descendants of Africa were actually cursed by God. Many people in the early part of the nineteenth and twentieth centuries (and some even to this day), point to that one passage to justify years of oppression and slavery of black people around the world. Many people felt they had a theological imperative to enslave black people in this and other countries. Some believed that those not coming from one of the lands founded by Shem and Japheth were cursed into slavery for all time—forced to be "slaves of slaves to their brothers." After all, "it could be found in the Bible!"

Despite the huge wealth of scriptural evidence clearly and emphatically against racism, oppression, and injustice, many will still use a phrase or a chapter from the Bible, out of context, in order to justify violence or oppression. Even with the powerful works of the prophets, the Gospels, and the writings of Paul and James, people sang out this passage regarding the sons of Ham for hundreds of years as a means of justifying oppression of others. A god who would doom generations of people into miserable slavery and bigotry might fit in with a god who would curse a king for showing mercy, or kill a world for disobedience. But would this kind of attitude fit the personality of a God who sent his Son to die for the sins of that same world? Which one of these two divergent personalities really belongs to this God? The one who would know best, is again, the one who knows God best—the Son himself.

> "All things have been given over to me by my Father. No one knows the Son except the Father, and no one knows the Father except the Son and all to whom the Son wishes to reveal him." (Matthew 11:27)

Jesus' description of God is quite different than the vengeful and jealous God sometimes portrayed in the Old Testament. Jesus speaks of a loving God and Father who only wants the best for his creation. His love is so great that he would go to any length to save them and to keep them from harm. He would even give up the one thing in his life that is even more important to him than creation itself, his only Son. Yet as we have seen, this God acts with love and mercy even when his Son is put to death.

And as if the "apple did not fall far from the tree," Jesus echoes the sentiments of the Father when he calls all to love and be merciful. If God appears to act in ways in the Old Testament that differ from the description of God in the New Testament, always trust the description given by Jesus.

No one knows the Father as does the Son nor knows the Son, as does the Father. If anyone interprets an act of nature as that of a vengeful and angry God, know that it does not square with a God who is full of love, and as noted earlier by John, is actually "love itself."

And if God is love, how does love behave? Again, Paul's definition is clearly quite descriptive, particularly:

> "Love is patient and kind. It is not full of envy nor is it loud and inflated. Love bears no rudeness and it is not self-seeking. Love is not quick to anger, nor does it sulk over wrongdoings. It does not rejoice in injustice but it finds joy in justice and truth. Love protects, believes, hopes, and endures all things."
> (1 Corinthians 13:4–7)

This doesn't quite sound like a God who would kill a whole world or condemn whole generations into brutal slavery because of the curious act of one man. Would not that kind of God inspire more fear than love? And yet John says perfect love drives out fear. Is God not truly perfect love? John also makes it clear that any interpretation of Scripture (both Old Testament and New Testament) that enables people to hate, no matter who they might be, does not know the God of Jesus Christ. This is because loving God and loving people of all colors and nationalities must go hand-in-hand.

> "We love because God first loved us. If anyone would dare say, 'I love God,' yet displays hate for his brother, he is a liar. Anyone who does not show love toward a seen brother cannot love an unseen God. This is the commandment he gave us, 'Whoever loves God also must love his brother.'" (1 John 4:19–21)

Killing in the Name of the Lord

Aside from feeling more comfortable when exploring the Scriptures, there is another reason to put into proper perspective the attitudes attributed towards God in the Old Testament. Few things have been as destructive in civilization as the people of God (by whatever name that God is called), killing in the name of that God. People from all over the world have been killed in the name of religion. Sometimes the numbers have risen into the hundreds of thousands. This has been done not only by ancient tribes and foreign religions, but it also happened even in the early days of our church as well. Any honest account of the Crusades will show that thousands of men, women, and children were killed in the Middle East in the name of God and Jesus Christ. Looking back on the venture today, it seems clear that the interest in starting the Crusades stemmed from more than mere religious concerns.

> "Furthermore, Europe's population was growing, its urban life was beginning to revive, and both long distance and local trade were gradually increasing. European human and economic resources could now support new enterprises on the scale of the Crusades. A growing population and more surplus wealth also meant greater demand for goods from elsewhere. European traders had always looked to the Mediterranean; now they sought greater control of the goods, routes, and profits. Thus worldly interests coincided with religious feelings about the Holy Land and the pope's newfound ability to mobilize and focus a great enterprise." (*Microsoft® Encarta® Reference Library 2003* © 1993–2002, Microsoft Corporation. All rights reserved.)

In other words, many historians believe that Europe had more than a religious reason to march into the Middle East. They also had economic reasons as well. Even more disturbing are the racial overtones connected to Crusades. Most people today reading the address of Pope Urban II (1042–1099) to the Franks (that is credited for spurring on the first Crusades) would cringe at the apparent racist language used to dehumanize those who were now occupying the Holy Land.

> "Oh, race of Franks, race from across the mountains, race beloved and chosen by God—as is clear from many of your works—set apart from all other nations by the situation of your country as well as by your Catholic faith and the honor which you render to the holy Church: to you our discourse is addressed . . ."

> "From the confines of Jerusalem and from the city of Constantinople a grievous report has gone forth and has repeatedly been brought to our ears; namely, that a race from

the kingdom of the Persians, an accursed race, a race wholly
alienated from God, 'a generation that set not their heart
aright, and whose spirit was not steadfast with God,' has vio-
lently invaded the lands of those Christians and has depopu-
lated them by pillage and fire." (From the Speech of Pope
Urban II at the Council of Claremont, 1095, [*Microsoft®
Encarta® Reference Library 2003* © 1993–2002, Microsoft
Corporation. All rights reserved.])

Whether or not it had been the intention of Pope Urban II, this type of
rhetoric undoubtedly prompted some to look upon the inhabitants of the
Holy Land as less than human, a race of people already cursed by God. Thus
slaughtering them may have been looked upon as something less heinous
than killing normal "blessed" human beings. As a result, men, woman, and
children were killed by the crusaders in the name of rescuing the holy city
from those who were less than holy.

"Siege of Jerusalem: The western European Christian armies
of the First Crusade surrounded the city of Jerusalem in June
1099. In mid-July, after a long siege, the crusaders took the
city by storm and massacred many of its inhabitants."
(*Microsoft® Encarta® Reference Library 2003* © 1993–2002,
Microsoft Corporation. All rights reserved.)

If one examined the Salem Witch Trials, it would be evident how at least
twenty people in Massachusetts (mainly woman) were tortured and killed in
the name of religion. But the trials in Salem were at the end of a much
greater witch hunting craze that began around the Renaissance and the
Reformation. From 1400–1700, thousands of people, again mostly woman,
were cruelly tortured and executed by men of religion, all in the name of
God. Much like the Crusades, the reasons for these actions can be traced
back historically (and in hindsight) to reasons not altogether sacred. These
include the sense of anxiety many orthodox church people felt with the coming of more scientific insight and the challenges of the Reformation. Many
people became frightened by a world that seemed to be spiraling out of control by such forces as science and this new form of religion known as
Protestantism.

"Later, the Reformation, the rise of science, and the emerging modern world—all challenges to traditional religion—created deep anxieties in the orthodox population. At the dawn of the Renaissance (15th century to 16th century) some of these developments began to coalesce into the "witch craze . . ." (*Microsoft® Encarta® Reference Library 2003* © 1993–2002, Microsoft Corporation. All rights reserved.)

Once again, men of religion were responsible for bringing order to all things. They were acting in ways that they assumed God would act considering their understanding of God's past performances. People were gathered up and killed by the thousands in the name of God. And the Gospel message of Jesus seems to be somewhere far in the distance. Right or wrong, many historians believe that Pope Innocent VIII (1432–1492) was responsible for starting the great witch-hunts of the fifteenth century.

"A major impetus for the hysteria was the papal bull *Summis Desiderantes* issued by Pope Innocent VIII in 1484. It was included as a preface in the book *Malleus Maleficarum* (The Hammer of Witches), published by two Dominican inquisitors in 1486. This work, characterized by a distinct anti-feminine tenor, vividly describes the satanic and sexual abominations of witches. The book was translated into many languages and went through many editions in both Catholic and Protestant countries, outselling all other books except the Bible." (*Microsoft® Encarta® Reference Library 2003* © 1993–2002, Microsoft Corporation. All rights reserved.)

There are many more such examples in history of people killing in the name of God. The reason I picked these two is that they were both done in the name of religion and were both filled with brutality as well as death. As mentioned earlier, most historians call the taking of Jerusalem by the Crusades as a massacre. The witch trials were brutal examples of unmitigated cruelty—with women being dunked into water to see if they would float. If they floated, they were considered to be witches and were put to death. If they drowned, they were deemed to be innocent.

How is it that church people could feel free to torture and kill people in the name of God? The answers are varied. But I believe one sure part of the answer can be traced to the idea that if God can act with harshness and even cruelty for the sake of some greater good, then surely those acting on God's behalf can act that way as well. After all, if God can destroy a whole world seemingly without mercy, surely those acting on God's behalf can destroy a city without mercy as well. If God can kill a woman such as Lott's wife simply because she turned around when told not to, surely the servants of God can kill women who were suspected of being agents of the devil. After all, it is not done for the sake of cruelty, but always for the greater good of the people of God. I believe that is one of the great and lingering dangers of anyone, especially Christians, keeping God locked in an ancient and primitive time and ignoring the powerful message of the New Testament. This danger increases when technology gives people the means to kill on even greater scale than before. Except for modern communism, atheists have waged few wars. Most kings and conquerors professed to believe in some form of deity. But when believers feel they can pattern their behavior on gods of little mercy or tolerance for others, explosive and deadly results can occur. Few acts of modern-day terrorism are conducted by "non-believers." Quite the contrary, religion is most often at the core of their actions.

God in the New and Wondrous Testament

For the Christian, understanding God in light of the New Testament is so important in an age of guns, bombs, and bullets. Christ who would not resort to violence, even unto death, became the Savior of the world. Love now becomes stronger than hate and also stronger than all of the world's guns, bombs, and bullets. This is the case *if* one accepts that overcoming hate through love and not violence is indeed the true way of God and of Jesus Christ. Believing that God still requires an eye for an eye—in a world filled with weapons of mass destruction—could lead to Armageddon, not from God but from his believers.

The first step in reading the Bible without fear is to understand the Old Testament without trying to make every facet of it make sense in a modern world. So many people shy away from reading the Old Testament because once they get started, they are struck with this image of a God who simply does not fit the image of the God of love they have come to know. In so doing, they miss some of the most beautiful and powerful writing in all of Scripture. They miss the heroic stories of men and women who made great sacrifices to follow God. They miss the powerful works of the prophets who constantly called people to love and justice. And they miss knowing a God so beautiful that the psalmist could not help but sing:

> "O God, my heart is steadfast and I will sing and joyfully make music with my whole soul. Be awake, harp and lyre! I will awaken the first light of morning. O LORD, I will offer you praise among the nations, I will sing your praises, O LORD, among all peoples. For your love is great, as high as the heavens. Your faithfulness abounds to the height of the skies. O God, high above the heavens, let your glory be over all the earth." (Psalm 108:2–6)

Ending Oppression and Injustice:
Love and Justice in the Language of the New Testament

The New Testament stresses that we are to love one another. It is from this love that all concern for those who are our neighbors must stem. Love and justice continue to work hand in hand, as though you cannot have one without the other. If there is love for Jesus, there must be action on behalf of the people that Jesus loves. Once again it is John, writing to the people who would be followers of Jesus, who sets down the prophetic dialogue between Jesus and Peter:

> "After breakfast, Jesus said to Simon Peter, 'Simon, son of John, do you love me more than all else?' 'Yes, Lord,' he responded, 'you know that I love you.' 'Then feed my lambs,' Christ said. A second time Christ asked, 'Simon, son of John, do you love me?' Simon replied, 'Yes, Lord, you know I love you.' 'Then tend my sheep.' A third time he queried, 'Simon, son of John, do you love me?' Simon Peter was concerned that Christ had said a third time, 'Do you love me?' and Simon Peter responded, 'Lord, you know everything and you know that I love you.' Jesus said, 'Feed my sheep.'" (John 21:15–17)

I believe that John intended for Christians see the inescapable relationship between love of God and service to God's people. Jesus, whom John already cites as the "Good Shepherd," tells Peter that the love he shows for him must be in direct proportion to the action he takes on behalf of his sheep. It is as though Jesus is trying to drive home the point by formulating a simple equation again and again until he is sure Peter gets the connection:

- Love me? Feed my lambs.
- Love me? Tend my sheep
- Love me? Feed my sheep.

The Old Testament writers would do the same thing, often equating answering God's call to fast and worship with action on behalf of one's neighbor:

- [What is it I, the LORD require of you?] . . . loose the fetter of injustice; untie the knots of the yoke...
- [What do I require?] . . . sharing your goods with the hungry, taking the homeless poor into your house...

■ [What is it I require?] . . . clothing the naked when you meet them, and never evading duty to your relatives. (cf. Isaiah 58:6–7)

In John's view, Scripture's whole thrust toward love and justice cannot be stressed too strongly. In fact, none of the New Testament authors ever tried to soften this theme. They used straightforward, no-nonsense talk when it came to justice. This connection between love of God and love of neighbor was so essential to biblical men and women that it bears repeating again. John said "to say one loves God while hating one's neighbor makes that person a liar," one of the strongest charges one person can level against another. (cf. John 4:19–20a)

The most fundamental principle of Christianity is to be found in the basic equation outlined above. It is the foundation of what is a single testament of thought that evolves from Genesis through Revelation. We see inescapable evidence that God stands against poverty, hunger, oppression, racism, powerlessness, and all the other things that make life for some of his people less than what it is for others. The evidence against hatred and oppression and the need for all God's people to actively work to overcome those injustices is overwhelming. The Bible also speaks on other matters, such as eschatology and the influence of the Holy Spirit, but it would be a mistake to believe that justice is merely a small facet of a greater message.

The Morality of Justice

Finally, before we can seek the moral messages the Bible has to teach us in this modern day, we need to get some understanding of the full meaning of what morality meant to the authors of the Scripture. According to the *New Webster's Dictionary* morality is:

> "Of a concern with the principles of right and wrong in conduct and character; teaching or upholding standards of good behavior; conforming to the rules of right conduct; ethics."

If the prophets are to be believed, God's morality (that is, principles, character, conduct, and standards of good behavior) is intricately tied to fairness, truth, and love. God could not be God if he did not love justice and hate oppression. God reveals his moral character again and again from the beginning to the end of Scripture. Because God breathes a part of himself into human creation—all human creation—he cannot love one part of that creation and hate another part. Would that not mean that he could hate the very breath of his being? Because God is a God of love, he must then love all of creation, which he has become a part of, in the same manner.

Perhaps then, one of the biblical writers' overall objectives and main concerns was to give future generations a book detailing the moral nature of a God whom they had come to know and love. He was a God that played an active role in their lives and their ongoing welfare. Perhaps those who wrote the later writings also aimed to create books that would never be outgrown, no matter how much technology and science advanced. They saw that the morality of God hadn't changed in the thousands of years since the first biblical writers began recording the Bible. By recording stories such as the one of the exodus experience, the ancient writers wanted all generations to see the folly of a people who might try to enforce standards of morality contrary to those of God. This is important to consider.

When one realizes that Egypt was one of the most technologically advanced civilizations in the world at the time of the Israelite exodus (believed by some to have been under the rule of Rameses II), then one can see a clear moral message taking shape. Egypt, with all its superior military might, was not able to stand against a group of slaves who sought what God demanded—freedom from oppression. When the Egyptians took it upon themselves to enslave the Israelites, God's sense of character and conduct was offended. His standard of behavior, right and wrong, was violated. God was forced to take sides because his very nature, character, and morality were assaulted. Oppression became a moral issue.

This idea also held true during the time of the New Testament. Rome was considered a great and technologically advanced civilization. One to two thousand years may have passed between the exodus experience and the life of Jesus. Yet Caesar and all of Rome could not stop a movement started by what appeared to be a local itinerant Rabbi and his small group of followers. What the authors of the New Testament were able to see was that humankind had not substantially changed morally in the thousand year span from Genesis to the time of their writings; this despite the technological advances they had witnessed in their own lifetime. Also, God's message remained the same relative to justice, freedom, oppression, and faith.

When Mahatma Gandhi (1869–1948) challenged the British in India in the 1930's and when the civil rights movement was beginning in this country in the 1960's, the concept that freedom from oppression was a moral issue became very clear. In both cases it was evident that a moral issue was stronger than anything modern technological forces could produce. Just as the Israelites faced Egypt and the early Christians faced Rome, the Indian people faced an empire in their own land. In the United States, African Americans faced a modern "army" in the South, only to emerge victorious. At that time there were often parallels drawn in sermons between the liberation of the Jews from the "Mighty Pharaoh" and a contemporary people overcoming racism and segregation. There were also parallels drawn between the ethics and morality of the Kingdom of God in contrast to the immorality of prejudice. In short, the civil rights movements here and in India were considered religious experiences. In fact, the whole idea of nonviolent resistance in this country's struggle to end segregation was derived from Dr. Martin Luther King, Jr. (1929–1968) and his perception of how the exodus experience and the early Christian experience had evolved. Coretta Scott King shares the words of her late husband:

"The religious tradition of the Negro has shown him that the nonviolent resistance of the early Christians had constituted a moral offensive of such overriding power that it shook the Roman Empire." (*The Words of Martin Luther King Jr.* [New York: Newmarket Press, 1983] p. 75)

Unfortunately, morality in the last few centuries has come to be linked with issues of sexuality alone. Consequently, this results in the larger, more total definition of morality often being obscured. It is easier to preach morality in the context of traditional western thought than it is to preach it in terms of justice and oppression. A perfect example of this is the infamous story of Sodom and Gomorrah. Until I began doing research for this book, I never associated the two towns with anything other than a story about what had become a very traditional definition of morality: a city that had become overrun with promiscuity and God said, "Enough already!" Yet we find that even a story like Sodom and Gomorrah is connected with the issue of injustice. It is namely the immorality of hunger, oppression, and the unwillingness to share with the poor:

"Consider the iniquity of your sister Sodom; she and her daughters had pride of wealth, abundant food, and great comfort, yet they never offered assistance to the wretched and the poor. They grew in haughtiness and did abominable deeds in my sight, and I removed them." (Ezekiel 16:49–50)

In the minds of people such as the prophets, those wishing to pattern their morality after God's cannot separate morality into such convenient compartments. God shows concern for the totality of the human person. His morality manifests itself in the whole of creation. Perhaps a God of justice, a God whose sensitivity was so outraged, whose character was so attacked, whose sense of right was so wronged, destroyed the city. Would it not be over the entire issue of immorality, an immorality that would have human beings treating other human beings in a way completely contrary to that which God himself had ordained?

"Administer justice each morning; rescue from the hand of the oppressor the one who has been oppressed; or my wrath will burst forth as a fire on account of the evil you have done, and it will burn with no one to quench it." (Jeremiah 21:12)

Drawing Proper Parallels

If the Bible is going to have any relevance on our moral thinking and on our code of social behavior, we must be able to identify with people. By this, I mean such people as the Pharisees, tax collectors, Roman centurions, and a host of other people from Scripture. At first glance they might seem a world apart from our society of today. Once we see that *they* were not that different from us, even though their *world* was very different from ours, we can begin to imagine the prophets and the Lord confronting us. We are confronted relative to our moral behavior when it comes to those oppressed by our contemporary society. On this point the Bible is ageless and there are no inconsistencies. If we are able to see the Pharisees as the religious leaders or clergy of the day, the Romans as the governing body of the land, and the centurions as the police or military, then without much difficulty we can draw a parallel between their time and ours. It gives us a tool to measure if our religious leaders are acting like Pharisees and if our political leaders are acting like Roman bureaucrats. If we can look at the Sanhedrin as the court system and see rich merchants as business and corporate heads, we can make a tie between their world and ours. We can then see where we would fit into that society as well as to ascertain how the lessons taught then might apply now. I believe understanding this is one of the most important elements of the Scriptures and of this book.

You Are There...

In the early 1960's Walter Cronkite hosted a clever television series called "You Are There." It featured popular historical events such as George Washington crossing the Delaware, or Julius Caesar's assassination, only this time you are present to witness it. At the beginning of the broadcast, Cronkite would say the words, "All things are now as they were then except, *you are there.*" I believe one of the most important overlooked functions of Scripture in modern society is the part that challenges us to put ourselves not just in the shoes of those who believed, but also in the shoes of those who didn't believe. In other words, to put *us* there, in the middle of those parables so that we might examine honestly how we would react to Jesus' message. For instance, how would most modern family-owned small business people believe they would have reacted to hearing the story of the prodigal son for the first time? Especially consider it if they did not know at the time that the story teller was in fact the son of God? Or how might a young entrepreneur react when, upon meeting Jesus, being told that if he wants true happiness, that he would have to sell everything and give it to the poor? Or how would a career military person react to being told by Jesus that the true way to peace was to love one's enemies and to turn the other cheek?

Upon hearing Gospel stories, people often proclaim how they would react differently if they had been there. The beauty of many of these stories is that if we take a step back, we can see that we *are* there. We might not be Pharisees or part of the Sanhedrin, but everyday people in our contemporary world fill today's equivalents of those professions. With the knowledge that Jesus really *was* and *is* the Son of God, we can look at those people in Scripture stories that did not believe. We can challenge ourselves as to whether we hold the same attitudes that prevented them from seeing and believing who Jesus really was. We ask ourselves if our attitudes conflict with those of Jesus. We will always be worse off for it if they do. Jesus is the Truth, the Light, and the Way; as long as we attempt to hold on to our own way of thinking over Christ's, true love and justice will always elude us.

What I would hope is that anyone reading this book will come away knowing that justice is not merely a passing thought in the Bible but is indeed one of its most fundamental concepts. It is a theme that constantly appears throughout the Bible. Granted, the Bible might leave room for generations to argue over whether the world was created in seven days or in seven billion years. However, it leaves very little room to argue over the important role that justice and love must play in the lives of believers.

It is also important to emphasize again that justice in the Bible directly addresses issues such as poverty, hunger, oppression, and racism. Justice is not to be mistaken for vengeance, which alone belongs to the Lord. It is possible to argue over matters of tradition *versus* matters of technology, but Christians must consider love and social justice to be fundamental components of their faith. If one were to take the question of whether or not social justice is essential to being a Christian into a court of law, with the Bible as testimony, the evidence would be overwhelmingly in favor of social justice. We can not hate our neighbors because of the color of their skin or feel no compassion for the poor and oppressed peoples of the world, while claiming to be followers of God. It is the same as believing in Christianity while denying the very existence of Christ.

Love and Justice are as Constant as God

There is divine wisdom in having the justice theme appear and reappear throughout the Bible. This says that love and justice are as constant as God, no matter the era or the people. Maybe the different generations of biblical writers, each in their own times, felt the need to reemphasize that faith without love and justice was indeed lifeless. Perhaps they wanted to warn their contemporaries and future generations that any religion based on this kind of lifeless faith would produce uncaring and lifeless believers. Dr. Martin Luther King, Jr. understood this. His wife again chronicles his words:

> "A religion true to its nature must also be concerned about man's social conditions. Religion deals with both earth and heaven; both time and eternity . . . the Christian Gospel is a two-way road. On the one hand, it seeks to change the souls of men and thereby unite with God; on the other hand, it seeks to change the environmental conditions of men so that the soul will have chance after it is changed. Any religion that professes to be concerned with the souls of men and is not concerned with the slums that damn them, the economic conditions that strangle them, and the social conditions that cripple them is a dry-as-dust religion." *(The Words of Martin Luther King Jr.*, p. 66)

And the scripture writers seldom tolerated people who refused to understand this most basic fact about the God of justice while claiming an allegiance to that same God. Ezekiel put it this way when he challenged his own people on this point. He tells God that even though they express devotion, they really are about their own greed, and care not for the poor. To paraphrase in modern language, it's as if he tells God that God might as well be whistling in the breeze. It's as if, even though God is speaking and they claim to be hearing, they refuse to "put their money where their mouths are."

> "My people come to you as they do; sitting before you to listen to your words, but they do not heed or practice them. They profess devotion with their mouths but their hearts are full of greed, seeking unjust gain. To them you are nothing more than a singer of love songs, with a pleasing voice and a skilled touch on an instrument. They hear your words but do not practice them." (Ezekiel 33:30–32)

In other words, he tells God, they just don't get it.

Human Nature

"There is no condemnation now for those who live in union with Christ Jesus. For the law of the Spirit, which brings us life in union with Christ Jesus, has set me free from the law of sin and death. What the law could not do, because human nature was weak, God did. He condemned sin in human nature by sending his own son, who came with a nature like man's sinful nature, to do away with sin. God did this so that the righteous demands of the law might be fully satisfied in us who live according to the spirit, and not according to human nature. Those who live their lives as their human nature tells them to have their minds controlled by what human nature wants. Those who live as the spirit tells them to, have their minds controlled by what the spirit wants. To be controlled by human nature results in death, to be controlled by the spirit results in life and peace. And so a person becomes an enemy of God when he is controlled by his human nature; for he does not obey God's law, and in fact he cannot obey it. Those who obey their human nature cannot please God." (Romans 8:1–8)

Paul makes a very powerful argument when he says that merely having the Law was not enough to make people live by it. Simply saying what *should* be done did not *get* it done. The Law could not be followed fully because he believes it is against our human nature to live as God and Christ would have us live. "What the Law could not do because human nature was weak..." (cf. Romans 8:3) Paul seems to know that hearing what Christ says are the solutions to many of the world's problems, not only seems unworkable, but even feels wrong. It would not be most human beings' natural reaction to, when being slapped on the face, to turn and present the other cheek. Our natural human response would be either to run away, or to retaliate. But yet "turning the other cheek" is according to Jesus, God's law. (cf. Matthew 5:39; Luke 6:29) Paul says the righteous demands of the Law could only be satisfied by those who live "according to the spirit," (Romans 8:4) and here he makes a very powerful point. He says that one has a choice to live either as their human nature leads them or according to the spirit. He says that to live by human nature alone means that they will be *controlled* by that nature. But those who live as the spirit tells them will have "their minds controlled by what the spirit wants." (Romans 8:5) If a person is to be controlled by one (human nature), the result is death; to be controlled by the other (spirit), the result is life.

In our contemporary society, the results of this can be seen in the area we call the Holy Land. The ongoing battles rage with both sides swearing to avenge the lives of those who were killed by the opposition. An "eye for an eye" (Matthew 5:38) seems to be the rule of the day, while turning the other cheek (Matthew 5:39) seems to be an unfathomable idea. While both sides of the conflict feel justified to respond with revenge and retaliation, the results have been utterly tragic, leaving death and mutilation on both sides. Yet, despite the death and chaos this kind of thinking has produced, neither side seems willing (at this stage in history) to turn the other cheek. It's as if feeling to do so would only produce more of what they are already experiencing.

But perhaps the most poignant point Paul makes is to say that a person becomes an "enemy of God" (Romans 8:7) if he does not allow the spirit to take control his life. Also in Romans 8:7, Paul writes that a person who is controlled by human nature does not obey God's law, "and in fact cannot obey it." And so repentance, i.e., turning away from the old ways of violence and retribution, is unobtainable without the spirit. Additionally, even the desire to repent is lessened by the fact that what is called for from God through Christ feels so unnatural to man's basic nature. One would be tempted to believe God must be asking for something else.

Lead us not into temptation, but deliver us from evil. (Matthew 6:13)

Paul says that if you truly belong to Christ and allow Christ to "live in you," then you will live according to what the spirit wants. That decision will result in life for the individual rather than death. And, if one submits totally to the spirit—rather than becoming enslaved by human weakness—one becomes truly free, a rather interesting paradox. Equally important is the reality that one ceases to be afraid, but instead becomes a child of God.

"But you do not live as your human nature tells you to; instead, you live as the spirit tells you to—if, in fact, God's Spirit lives in you. Whoever does not have the Spirit of Christ does not belong to him. But if Christ lives in you, the Spirit is life for you because you have been put right with God, even though your bodies are going to die because of sin. If the Spirit of God, who raised Jesus from death, lives in you, then he who raised Christ from death will also give life to your mortal bodies by the presence of the holy Spirit. So then my brothers, we have an obligation to not live as our human nature wants us to. For if you live according to your human nature, you are going to die; but if by the spirit you put to death your sinful actions, you will live. Those who are led by God's Spirit are God's sons. For the Spirit that God has given you does not make you slaves and cause you to be afraid; instead, the Spirit makes you God's children, and by the Spirit's power we cry out to God, "Father! My Father!" (Romans 8:9–15)

Again the point needs to be stressed that there is a huge difference between hearing the Lord's call to live life in accordance with Christ's wishes (and trying to follow those commands) versus hearing what the Lord has to say and saying "no." If turning the other cheek is hard, Jesus tells us that he will help us get from where we are to where he wants us to be, no matter how hard that may seem. Jesus promises to send the help of the Spirit to bring about gargantuan changes in our actions and attitudes *if* we submit to his rule. However, Jesus can do very little to help us if one hears his words and decides it is *not* what one wish to do. Jesus will not alter his commands in order to make it easier for the world to obey them. Nevertheless, he will send spiritual help and guidance to all who would faithfully say "yes" to his ways. Wishes and saying "yes" (even if one fails), versus hearing those commands and deciding the Lord is wrong can be the difference in accepting Jesus as one's Lord.

Understanding this helps us to see how the Spirit applies itself not only to all the social justice commands of God, but to matters of war and retribution as well. Loving one's neighbor (even though that neighbor seems different on the surface), caring for people who are poor (even though you may not know them personally), or actively getting involved in causes that combat oppression and hunger (not only at home, but also in lands that are thousands of miles away), may all seem like things outside of the scope of one's normal way of life. But Christ tells us we must not only care, but we must also be actively involved in those issues— since the affected people are *related to us through Jesus*. The Lord tells us that *he is* that person who is hungry, in prison, naked, or thirsty. And while these people might *seem* like strangers to us, through the Spirit their identities become known to us and the solutions to their problems become known as well. We will be able to leap beyond the limits of our natural desire which would have us take care of simply our own needs. Instead, we'll begin to truly see the whole world as a family that is interconnected by the God of all life, and the Spirit who is Lord and giver of life.

Through the Spirit we can also break free from the recurring cycle of violence so prevalent in the world. Without the Spirit's help, we find ourselves in a continuing state of what Philip Yancy calls "un-grace." In his wonderful book *What's so Amazing About Grace?* one of his chapters is about what he calls "An Un-Natural Act," that is, forgoing the urge for vengeance and violence in favor of what Christ tells us is the way God would have us (according to the Spirit) live with one another.

> "I have told the story of one family that spans a century of ungrace. In world history similar stories span many centuries, with far worse consequences. If you ask a bomb-throwing teenager in Northern Ireland or a machete-wielding soldier in Rwanda or a sniper in the former Yugoslavia why they are killing, they may not even know. Ireland is still seeking revenge for atrocities Oliver Cromwell committed in the seventeenth century; Rwanda and Burundi are carrying on tribal feuds that extend long past anyone's memory; Yugoslavia is avenging memories from World War II and trying to prevent a replay of what happened six decades ago.
>
> Ungrace plays like the background static of life for families, nations, and institutions. It is sadly, our natural human state."
> (*What's so Amazing About Grace?* [Grand Rapids, MI: Zondervan Publishing Co., 1997] cf. p. 83)

While it is obvious that in the time that has elapsed since Philip Yancy wrote this chapter, some of those conflicts have been resolved. Still his point is well taken, and clearly so is Paul's. When I read what Yancy wrote, I could not help but hear Paul's words ringing in my mind:

> "So then my brothers, we have an obligation to not live as our human nature wants us to. For if you live according to your human nature, you are going to die; but if by the spirit you put to death your sinful actions, you will live." (Romans 8:12)

As well as hearing him say:

> "For the spirit that God has given you does not make you slaves and cause you to be afraid . . ." (Romans 8:15)

It Is Only through Grace

And so Paul tells us that the only way we will ever break out of the violence, the mistrust, and the injustices that foster so much of the world's misery, is to live as Jesus tells us to live. We are to know that it is not a mistake, a misprint, or a bad translation when Jesus tells us to love those who hate us and not to repay violence with more violence. But he warns us that we will delude ourselves into thinking that when it comes justice and tolerance, Jesus was speaking perhaps metaphorically and not literally. It is only through the grace and the Spirit of God that we can begin to see that Christ is speaking a reality—that without that the Spirit will remain too distant for most to ever comprehend. However, without that vital comprehension, Jesus remains an object of worship alone rather than a leader to be followed. As history has taught us, it is always easier to worship than it is to follow.

See website

904 777-
1135